MW01520250

Creating Connections

How Friendships Feed the Soul

Joyce,
So glad to make
a connection with
a fellow Canuck.
Enjoy these stories!
♡ Nicole —Nov
2024

NICOLE VAN KUPPEVELD

ALONG WITH 21 INSPIRING STORYTELLERS

© 2024 ALL RIGHTS RESERVED.

Published by She Rises Studios Publishing **www.SheRisesStudios.com.**

No part of this book may be reproduced or transmitted in any form whatsoever, electronic, or mechanical, including photocopying, recording, or by any informational storage or retrieval system without the expressed written, dated and signed permission from the publisher and primary author.

LIMITS OF LIABILITY/DISCLAIMER OF WARRANTY:

The co-authors and publisher of this book have used their best efforts in preparing this material. While every attempt has been made to verify the information provided in this book, neither the co-authors nor the publisher assumes any responsibility for any errors, omissions, or inaccuracies.

The co-authors and publisher make no representation or warranties with respect to the accuracy, applicability, or completeness of the contents of this book. They disclaim any warranties (expressed or implied), merchantability, or for any purpose. The co-authors and publisher shall in no event be held liable for any loss or other damages, including but not limited to special, incidental, consequential, or other damages.

ISBN: 978-1-964619-41-5

Dedication

Louise Guay

My first friend, my mum, who has through her deep and meaningful friendships taught me how to cultivate those types of friendships in my life, including the one we share today as not only mother:daughter but adult friends.

And for…

Anyone who is looking to cultivate, nurture and sustain the kinds of friendships shared in this anthology.

Friendship is a tapestry woven from shared experiences, tears, laughter and love.

—Nicole van Kuppeveld

TABLE OF CONTENTS

Foreword

The average Facebook user has 338 friends, according to <u>Brandwatch</u> and other social media watchers. I have 361 Facebook friends, so I must be really popular.

But as most of us understand, Facebook friends are followers; most aren't close friends. Most users consider only 28 per cent of all those connections to be genuine or close friends, and we'd turn to just four of them in a crisis, according to a University of Oxford study. And let's face it — if you can't turn to someone in a crisis, that's not true friendship.

Younger people tend not to use Facebook as much — they are on social media platforms like Instagram, TikTok and Snapchat. These virtual communities with virtual friends might be satisfying to some, but the connections often aren't deep and many people long for more.

A real friend — one you share a deep and meaningful relationship with — is someone who is there for and with you in good times and bad. They're someone you can call at 7 a.m. to tell them about a weird dream you had last night, or at 2 a.m. when your crippling anxiety won't let you sleep. You can get together when you haven't washed your hair, plucked your eyebrows or even gotten out of your pyjamas, and they won't say a word. They may not live in the same neighbourhood, the same city or even the same country, but when you talk or text or email, it's like they're in the same room, sharing a glass of wine.

Those are the kinds of friendships we all want — and need — but many of us have trouble building and maintaining them. The May 2021 American Perspectives Survey found that Americans report having fewer close friendships than they once did, talking to their friends less often, and relying less on their friends for personal support. There's no reason to believe things are any better in Canada.

Another series of U.S. surveys carried out in 2022 and 2023, called the American Friendship Project, found that while 75-per-cent of those surveyed were satisfied with the number of friends they had, they weren't happy with the amount of time they spent with those friends. Forty per cent wanted more close connections. Thirty-six per cent said they had trouble maintaining friendships, and half said it was difficult to make new friends.

Some experts call this a friendship recession or a friendship crisis. Whatever we call it, it's a serious problem that affects people of all ages, backgrounds, ethnicities and gender.

Why is this happening?

We are a mobile society and the economy is challenging, so many people move around for jobs, opportunities and better housing options — leaving childhood, university and workplace friends behind.

It would also be easy to blame the friendship recession on a lack of work-life harmony and a shortage of time to focus on friends. But in many industrialized countries, including Canada, people are actually working fewer hours than they did in the past. Still, we all feel stressed — about our jobs, our responsibilities, our families. As a result, many of us are coming home from work and socializing less, spending more of our precious time on screens — laptops, smartphones, televisions. Maybe we're even watching reruns of Friends and marvelling at how close those beautiful New Yorkers were.

Some people blame COVID-19, and certainly, being isolated and unable to interact in person took a huge toll on friendships during the pandemic. And in the post-COVID world, we can't even rely on making friends at the office as we did in the past, now that so many people are working remotely with colleagues they may never meet.

Indeed, so many of us have trouble making and keeping friends, there's a new term for it — friendship anxiety. Even if you have friends, you may be stressing over whether they actually like you or whether they're going to drop you for someone less needy. It's not a clinically recognized condition (yet) but if you're on TikTok, you'll see lots of people sharing stories of their friendship anxiety.

The bottom line: Many of us are no longer prioritizing friendships. As a result, long-time relationships may wither and die, and many of our remaining friendships may feel shallow and superficial. And making new friends — real friends — seems like a lost art. Keeping them is another challenge.

Why does it matter?

Not everybody needs a lot of close friends, but we all need at least a few. Those without friends are more likely to feel lonely, which can have profound impacts on their physical and mental health. A report by Women's College Hospital in Toronto found that an epidemic of loneliness is rapidly spreading across Canada, with seniors and marginalized people at the highest risk. More than a third of older Canadians report that they feel lonely at least some of the time, according to Statistics Canada.

In the U.S., the Surgeon General called loneliness, isolation and lack of connection a public health crisis in May 2023.

Lonely people are at higher risk of depression and anxiety. They often suffer from poor sleep, which is linked to poor cardiovascular health. Chronic loneliness and social isolation significantly increase a person's risk of premature death — a risk that may rival smoking, obesity and physical inactivity.

It's not an exaggeration to say having close friends could save your life.

What can you do about it?

Like everything else that's worthwhile in life, making and keeping friends takes work, sometimes a lot of work. There's no magic potion, no fairy dust you sprinkle over an acquaintance to turn her into a lifelong friend. It's not like those girls who showed up at summer camp and had seven best friends by the time the first campfire was lit. (Of course, other girls spent all their time reading comic books on their top bunks, unable to make any new friends.)

If you Google "how to make friends self-help books," you'll find dozens of offerings. Find Your People. Why Has Nobody Told Me This Before? Platonic: How the Science of Attachment Can Help You Make — and Keep — Friends. If you're having trouble making or keeping close friendships, you should read some of these books.

And check out the various lists online, with tips about making friends. Volunteer. Join a sports team. Check out MeetUp. Go to church. Take your dog to the dog park. All good suggestions.

This wonderful book, Creating Connections: How Friendships Feed the Soul, isn't a self-help guide and it doesn't have lists of tips and advice. But it is a remarkable resource, full of wisdom, inspiration and love, in stories of friendship shared by 20 women and one man who are lucky enough to be in the village built over many years by the anthology's amazing creator, Nicole van Kuppeveld.

Nicole's goal, with Creating Connections: How Friendships Feed the Soul, was to reach out to people who are struggling with friendship to teach them how to create the kinds of deep, soul-affirming relationships she has worked so hard to maintain over her lifetime. She insisted that this book wasn't to be about her. It was to be about her relationships — how they happened, how they've grown, how they nurtured her and made her the strong woman and leader she is today.

I think you'll cry when you read some of these stories, and you'll definitely laugh. And I'm confident you'll learn something you can use in your own life, with your own friends, both new and old.

Bestselling American novelist Morgan Matson, who writes for kids and teens, shares this wisdom: "Real friends are the ones you can count on no matter what. The ones who go into the forest to find you and bring you home. And real friends never have to tell you that they're your friends."

Nicole will never be lost in the woods for very long. Her friends would never let that happen.

—Keri Sweetman

Keri Sweetman

Motivational Writing Coach, Editor, and Friend
Journalist

https://www.linkedin.com/in/keri-sweetman-8aa6b412/
https://www.facebook.com/keri.sweetman

I was born in Quebec but spent most of my childhood and early adult years in Ottawa, where I married in 1980. David and I raised three wonderful children there, before moving to Edmonton in 1998. Edmonton feels like home now, but I'm still drawn back to Ontario, to our family cottage on the edge of Algonquin Park.

David and I were both journalists – we met at a media tour of the Pickering nuclear station (and the sparks flew!) My career included stints at Canadian Press, the Ottawa Citizen and the Edmonton Journal. I was widowed in 2018 and wouldn't have made it through that tough time without my amazing friends, some of whom I've known for more than 40 years.

My greatest joy is my family – a son and daughter in Edmonton and a son in Toronto – and the additional blessing of two precious grandbabies, both born in 2023.

Author's Note

My earliest memories are of spending time in both of my grandmothers' kitchens, with aunties and cousins cooking and sharing the stories of our lives.

Both of my grand-mémères were strong women who raised their children in a matriarchal environment. Although my mother was a Caucasian woman, she was adopted into a Métis family, so my mother's sisters educated me in the Indigenous ways of knowing, without my knowing. This is truly where my woman-woman relationships were formed and bonds were sealed.

I've been blessed with a circle of friends that I've met and kept over many decades, some from grade school. I fondly refer to them as the GEMS in my collection. I am honoured that some of them agreed to share their personal friendship experiences to inspire our readers.

Each co-author shares his or her unique perspective, exploring the evolution of friendships from casual acquaintances to profound connections. Together, they reveal essential qualities that define true friendship, offering insights into how to nurture and sustain these invaluable bonds throughout adulthood.

The tales within these pages are not just reflections of individual experiences; they are a collective celebration of the beauty and strength that friendships bring to our lives. You'll discover laughter, vulnerability and the shared understanding that we all seek connection in our own ways.

Whether you're looking to forge new friendships or strengthen those you already hold dear, let *Creating Connections: How Friendships Feed the Soul* illuminate your path toward richer, more fulfilling relationships.

I invite you to join us on this journey and discover how friendships can truly feed your soul.

Warm regards,
Nicole van Kuppeveld

Nicole van Kuppeveld

Organizations by Design Inc.
Founding Partner
Entrepreneur, Facilitator, Leadership Coach, Author and Friend

https://www.linkedin.com/in/nicole-van-kuppeveld-6371069a/
https://www.facebook.com/nicole.vankuppeveld.5
https://www.instagram.com/organizationsbydesigninc/
https://www.organizationsbydesign.ca/
https://creatingconnectionsfriendshipsthatfeedthesoul.ca/

A lifelong cultivator of deep connections, I have woven a rich tapestry of friendships that have shaped my life. Being a daughter, a wife, mother, grandmother, entrepreneur and volunteer have enriched my understanding of the bonds that shape us.

Inspired by the personal stories of extraordinary women (and a few remarkable men) in my life, this anthology offers readers a glimpse into the hearts and minds of those who understand the enduring power of friendship. I am honoured to have curated and co-authored this anthology with 21 of the GEMS in my friendship collection.

My professional experience as a leadership expert has deepened my appreciation for the role of relationship and connection in our professional growth. As the founding partner of Organizations by Design Inc., a leadership consultancy firm, I empower women to lead with authenticity and to harness their collective power through woman-centred coaching and leadership development practices.

Cultivating

I. Cultivating

True friendships bring women together, heart to heart and soul to soul. It is in these spaces that we witness each other's beauty, strength, vulnerability, intellect, courage, compassion, generosity and talents. We are challenged, supported and encouraged to learn and grow from this deep connection, supporting each other to be, and to become, our best selves.
—Karen Caine

If one has friends from many walks of life, it is very rewarding and never boring.
—Michelle Hlady

From my perspective, friendship truly starts with ourselves. Meaningful relationships, including friendships, are about being authentic and vulnerable, coming from a place of love (appreciation, acceptance, compassion, etc.) instead of fear (which can show up in emotions such as jealousy, anger, expectations, etc). As I grow older, I am also beginning to understand the importance of having various kinds of friendships as a woman...and having various friends from different age groups.
—Wanda Polzin Holman

If you want to be a good friend, pick good friends.
—Sue Timanson

Be kind to one another. Stop and take the time to listen to people. Engage in conversation. You will meet people from all walks of life. You never know who will become your new best friend.
—Jody McCoppen

Seeking Connections: Being True to Yourself

Nicole van Kuppeveld

I believe that people come into my life to teach me lessons that I still need to learn. Lessons about how to be the best version of myself. About how to be in relationships. About what's really important. And about how to live my best life — every moment of each day.

I show up in life every day in a way that attracts people who have the potential to become friends. In my initial encounters with people, I am seeking depth, authenticity, shared passion, adventure, learning and a love of life. These are the most important qualities that I seek to create deep and lasting friendships.

Depth

I seek out and befriend women who have depth of character. Although some of my close friends might have beautiful nails that are important to them, or won't miss a monthly eyelash appointment, a common characteristic they share is a willingness to bring a depth of conversation, perspective, ideas and experiences to our friendship. Individuals who easily move beyond the superficial to share their character, passions and life experiences. Women who bring their whole selves into the relationship.

Karen is a great example of a friend who brings every part of herself into our friendship, which started when she returned from a sabbatical I was covering at a non-profit agency. Simultaneously, I was asked to extend my client contract and we became 'officemates.' We connected quickly and our relationship deepened as we experienced and embraced both professional and personal experiences, including the death of my brother by suicide.

Our relationship blossomed into one of deep trust where we generated solutions to complex work challenges, shared our struggles, celebrated our individual and team accomplishments — and most importantly, connected at an emotional level, becoming very attuned to how our work was impacting us.

We complement one another perfectly and our professional relationship extended into a business relationship. Following her retirement from the non-profit agency, Karen joined my leadership consultancy, Organizations by Design Inc. (OBD) and was instrumental in building the foundation, philosophy and unique approach to leadership development for women leaders. Although Karen has gone into full-time retirement, we maintain a deep friendship. I appreciate the depth of listening and inquiry that Karen continues to provide as a 'thinking partner' when we connect to catch up on our lives, and my heartwork.

Authenticity

Authenticity is one of the essential qualities to attracting friends who will stay around through the good times and the bad and all the times in between. Showing up and showing others who you are is critical to connecting with people at a deep level.

I've been told that my authenticity is one of the most important qualities I bring to my friendships. My ability to be authentic about where I am at, the position that I have on an issue, and what I am experiencing in my life allows others to truly see me in that moment. I expect the same from my friends. I want them to let me know and see where they are in the moment, whether that be struggling with a key relationship, not feeling motivated in their work or being elated about the arrival of a new grandchild.

It's like finding an organization that is the 'right fit' for you. A place where you have a connection to the people, work culture, shared values and passion for the work. A place where you feel valued and respected for the skills and qualities you bring to the work. Where you feel like you are an integral part of the team and are making significant contributions to the mission and vision of the organization. And most importantly, where you feel 'psychologically safe' to be who you are and to share your inputs without fear of reprisal. This is the same 'fit' that you find in a friendship that is meant to be a long and lasting one.

Authenticity is best exhibited in my friendship with Nancy, who is an integral part of 'my village.' Nancy and I initially met when we were volunteer Girl Guide Leaders. Our deep friendship was forged when she said 'yes' to being the communications director when I ran as a candidate in a municipal election campaign.

It was during that campaign that we had the opportunity to 'see and be' our authentic selves. You really see who the other person is when they have worked an eight-hour day at their job, door-knocked for four hours, and then connect to review campaign communications at 10 p.m. after a 15-hour day. You get to know what that other person is made of — their dedication, skill set and commitment — either as the candidate or as someone in a critical campaign role. There is no hiding your thoughts, ideas or emotions during the frenzy of a campaign. In my municipal campaign, Nancy was 'the voice of the candidate.' She prepared my policy positions, media ads, social media posts and forum preparation. She got to see inside my head. As we finessed the messaging, I got to see inside her head as well. We got to see one another's character, brilliance and dedication.

We have continued to be there for each other during the transitions and phases of our lives, from preparing and releasing our adult children into the world to releasing beloved family members and a mutual friend to a better world, to supporting quietly during emotional times and celebrating the blessings in our lives. We've also had hard conversations that come from a place of deep love, good intentions and caring. And we have a lot of fun, and drink wine together!

Shared passion

In 1993, I became a member of a women's service organization, which was a place where I met several women who remain very close friends years after our active service. One of these women, Kim, became one of my closest friends.

The year we met was 2000. At that time, she was on leave from our service organization, the Junior League of Edmonton, recovering from a postpartum surgical procedure. I was assigned as her placement adviser. As we got to know each other, we quickly discovered that we shared many passions: family, learning, fitness, travel and volunteerism. But it was our passion for politics that fanned the flame of our friendship.

Throughout our 24-year friendship, we have volunteered for many political campaigns at the local, provincial (state) and federal levels. We worked as campaign volunteers and then later as candidates in our respective local council and mayoral campaigns. So many adventures on so many campaign trails solidified our friendship during and between campaigns. Even today, it is rare for the 'politics of the day' not to be broached in our phone conversations or during dinner parties.

We have shared all the big moments and cherished the small moments in our lives over the years. Our other shared passions have been a source of connection and resulted in a close friendship as two couples who like to travel. We have celebrated special occasions, like their 25th anniversary in Las Vegas and our 35th in Austria on a bike and boat tour. Our shared passion for travel extended to our children, when we embarked on a three-week European vacation with both of our families.

Meeting a friend through a shared passion provides an opportunity to build experiences and get to know each other. So although not everyone in the service organization or the political campaign you join will become a close friend, it is a great opportunity to find someone you connect with and a good starting point to build a friendship. Kim is that person who reminds me of who I am when I sometimes forget; she is my champion and my go-to person when my world is falling apart. I am her person during those dark nights we all face periodically in our lives. I am there when she feels the sky is falling, to assure her that everything will be alright and that this too shall pass. We remind each other that as long as we have each other — and others we love — that's all we need. We hold space for one another until we find ourselves and are ready to carry on.

Kim and I illuminate each other's brilliance and accept our imperfections, in each and every moment.

Adventure

We were young adults experimenting with our newfound independence. We were university students, working part-time jobs and seeking new experiences in all aspects of our lives.

Both of us had signed up for a rafting trip down the beautiful Mackenzie and Fraser Rivers in the Rocky Mountains of Western Canada. We were paired up as roommates in a room with a double bed. The first morning we woke up, in a scene from Planes, Trains and Automobiles, with our lower right and left calves, respectively, stuck together. We burst into laughter. Perhaps that was the moment when our friendship adventure began.

During that same trip, I jumped off a train trestle into the river at a spot our rafting guide identified as safe. As a lifeguard and swim instructor, I initiated my 'V sit' a moment too early and my tailbone made first contact with the water. It was Shannon who swam out to pull me in, having temporarily lost sensation in my legs, and she found a hemorrhoid ring that I sat on for the rest of the trip. To this day, we are still surprised that this item would be available for a young adult river trip.

After graduating from the University of Alberta, we took another trip, this time to Mexico, not long before I was to get married. As the bride-to-be and with her as my maid of honour, it was a chance to get away before the wedding. More adventures ensued, including a full-body sunburn and food poisoning. Me, with the sunburn, with Shannon applying Noxzema from head to toe. And Shannon with food poisoning during the trip home that she likes to forget. Never a dull moment when travelling with Shannon!

Our adventures turned to local shopping trips and our annual November birthday dinners, during those years we were working professional jobs and I was raising a family. Our travel adventures resumed in the summer of 2023 when Shannon joined us on a bike and boat cruise through Austria to help celebrate our 35th wedding anniversary. There are more travel, shopping and dinner adventures on the horizon, like that Wild Women in Antarctica trip that keeps coming into my social media feed.

Having fun and going on adventures with Shannon has created memories that last a lifetime and a friendship that has withstood the test of time. The kind of friendship that for several years would be rekindled only once annually at our joint birthday celebrations in November.

Regardless of the time that has passed since our last visit, we pick up where we last left off. Those adventures, both past and future, keep our friendship spirited and fun.

Learning

I was 10 years old and was transferred as a result of the redistribution of students to a new school, where Monica was the principal's daughter. A perfect friendship for a keen student and consummate learner like me to pursue.

In my version of the story, we had sworn our allegiance to being best friends in no time at all, yet we were inclusive and opened up our friendship circle to include others. As childhood friends, we got to experience so many new things together. Over the past 49 years, we have continued to learn about and from each other, as well as experiencing many new activities together, having travelled through the many phases of our lives. First as elementary and junior high school friends, then as young independent university students, then as parents and now as grandmothers.

I learned a lot about family, food and heritage from Monica. I am grateful not only for Monica but for her family's influence in supporting me in becoming the woman I am today. Monica comes from a family with strong values, faith and cultural roots. It would not be until decades later, when my mother learned that her birth mother had come from Ukrainian heritage, that my love of the ethnic culinary dishes that we devoured at special celebrations with Monica's family would make sense! My fondest memories of Monica's mother are her wit, her dedication to family, her cooking and her championing of my political aspirations, including her unwavering commitment as a volunteer on the campaign trail.

I also learned a lot about parenting as Monica started her family first and was a role model. I adopted many of her parenting practices and learned from her successes, trials and errors. I credit her with developing my parenting philosophy focused on unconditional love, a lot of adventure, fun, and celebrating special occasions and milestones.

And providing our children with opportunities and experiences to support them in becoming the people they are meant to be. Preparing them to go out into the world, encouraging them to share the gift of themselves, to experience life to the fullest, to love deeply and to live responsibly.

I learned the value of a deep friendship. The gift of a longstanding relationship with someone who loves you and knows you sometimes better than you know yourself. Someone who has witnessed you grow and become the person you are today. The value of someone who can hold space for you during your darkest moments and dance with you during the most joyful ones. Someone who celebrates you and can see your brilliance and imperfections in the same moment, and still love you intensely, without reservation.

In these types of friendships, we give one another permission to say things that the other person needs to hear, truths that might be hard to hear, knowing they always come from a place of caring and the best intentions. Sometimes we are not able to see aspects of ourselves and we need friends who can be truth tellers. Having those things brought to light can help us get unstuck, release us and allow us to find a path forward.

I learned that the strongest friendships ebb and flow. Although our partners, family and work have taken the forefront at times over the past five decades, we can always connect at a very deep and personal level. That was evidenced by a recent conversation following a 'Sip & See' we hosted so our friends could meet our first grandson. After the last guests departed, Monica and I settled into a three-hour conversation about the status of our marriages and our plans for the future. Time stood still. We were fully present in the moment. There was deep and personal mutual sharing, with the raw emotions that accompanied them. We shared things that no other human will ever know.

We share an ability to be fully open and vulnerable with each other, knowing that the sanctity of our longstanding relationship will be able to hold a space to sustain the depth of the hurt, the breadth of our caring and the hope for our respective futures. Our conversation once again reinforced that those bonds that we have built continue to stand the test of time as we continue to navigate our journey into another decade of our lives.

Having this kind of friendship is priceless. As such, Monica is one of the most precious gems in my friendship collection.

A love of life

We began as colleagues, our paths intersecting in the demanding world of a vibrant community college. Tracy's extraordinary intellect, unwavering determination and infectious enthusiasm were evident in her job interview. She was a force to behold: a woman who filled the room with her presence. She was feisty and fiercely loyal. But what truly set her apart was how she showed up every day full of life — ready to take on whatever the day had to offer.

Our work in the executive suite was fast-paced and intense, requiring an ability to stay ahead of the curve, to create exceptional work under tight timelines, and to be able to handle feedback and pivot quickly to meet the relentless daily demands. Our friendship was forged through putting out fires and resolving conflict, and we emerged stronger and more resilient with each challenge. Yet not a day went by where we did not share a laugh. This made the stressful workplace fun.

Over the years, our conversations have been a constant source of support, inspiration and mutual growth. Our deep connection and bond have been instrumental in helping us both overcome obstacles and reach new heights. The idea of a sister from another mister perfectly encapsulates our unique bond. It's a bond built on mutual respect, trust, loyalty and an unwavering commitment to each other's success.

Tracy is so full of life! I love the energy that she exudes. Her passion and joie-de-vivre are abundantly evident whenever we get a chance to have a long conversation by phone (due to the distance between us) or when we connect face to face. We share a wicked sense of humour and a lot of laughs. I honestly cannot recall a conversation where we did not laugh so hard we cried, usually after one of us recounted a story where we laughed at ourselves. We fill each other's cup with love and laughter to sustain us until we next connect or meet up.

Tracy embodies that feisty, fierce love of life that is shared by all of my friends to varying degrees, but she is the gold standard in this category.

Forty-Nine Years and Counting:
The Enduring Magic of a True Connection

Monica Blackmore

This fall, I celebrated my 60th birthday at a party with my sisters and girlfriends in my beautiful backyard. A sleepover party when you turn 60 is not like a sleepover party when you are a teenager. You can't drink or stay up all night. Or perhaps you can...

I grew up on an acreage just outside of Sherwood Park. Nicole and I had many sleepovers at each other's houses while growing up.

When I turned 17, a few of us 'camped' at my acreage in the back field behind the house. We drank — of course we drank — and it went well into the night. At some point, we encountered a problem and didn't know what to do with the empty vodka bottle. Nicole took it upon herself to solve the problem and was brave enough to wade into the slimy slough and bury the vodka bottle in the sludge with her feet. What a champ! What determination! She must have done a great job as I am sure if that bottle eventually had surfaced, or if my dad had found it even years later, there would have been an interrogation. Luckily, Nicole and I have come a long way since then.

I wanted to start this story of my friendship with Nicole using that snippet about how badass, determined, resourceful, and full of confidence she was — and showcase her exceptional leadership skills even when we were teenagers.

We met in Grade 6, in the fall of 1975, which makes 2024 our 49th anniversary of knowing one another. That is the year that Nicole and I started at the same elementary school. My dad moved me and my siblings to this school when he began as principal there. Our teacher's name was Miss 'J', and she was not very good. At one point, Nicole made some smart-ass comment under her breath regarding something the teacher had said, and the teacher got quite angry, and Nicole was in trouble. Nicole did not like her, and I don't think the teacher liked Nicole either.

I was not immediately drawn to Nicole. Grade 6 girls can be so fickle. Nicole always talked about babysitting and making money, and I did not yet babysit as I lived on the acreage, making it difficult to get babysitting jobs. I thought that was so unfair. She was too confident and outgoing, and perhaps as I was quite sensitive, at that time she seemed too much.

When we became friends, I remember Nicole was confident and rather cool. She took no guff from anyone and could be a bit intimidating. She certainly spoke her mind. There were a few different groups of girls, and friends came and went, but she and I always stayed together.

In Grade 8, we were both pursuing swimming, and both ended up teaching swimming and lifeguarding through high school and university. Our weekend socializing centred around our work friends.

We went to many friends' parties in junior high and high school, attended school dances, and hosted gatherings and parties at our homes. Nicole had many steady boyfriends but still, she let me tag along so we could hang out (possibly much to the chagrin of her boyfriend).

Nicole had (and still has) a great sense of humour, so she was a lot of fun to hang out with. Sometimes she can also really poke fun at herself, which is quite funny.

Nicole had the not-so-brilliant idea of leaving high school to do her Grade 12 year elsewhere, so that year I would see her in the evenings or mostly on weekends. Her mom, Louise, or Mamma Guay whom she was so affectionately called, was like another mom to me. She was always excited to show me what she got for Nicole for her birthday and

Christmas ahead of time, and I was included in family dinners and events, and was always welcome to stay.

Nicole's dad, Andy, was always good for a laugh — or teasing us as we did silly teenage things. I love Nicole's parents as my own and enjoyed spending time there in my high school and university years. Nicole was always welcome at my home as well. My parents were very fond of her, and she too was always welcome for dinner, attended family functions, and met my extended family many times.

Nicole and I also drove to university together starting in the fall of 1982. We only had one or two classes together as we were studying in different faculties. I would drive and she would study in the car on the way to school, and still do well on the exam.

She was so busy with boyfriends and working that she always ended up finishing her term papers at the very last minute, usually with her mom or me doing the night-before-deadline typing. Her mom and I would wonder how she could be so last-minute, but she always pulled it off! Nicole always did well at school and went on to do great things.

I admire Nicole's determination and ability to organize and bring people together. She developed amazing leadership skills and did things that I could not have done. She does exude attitude — in a good way (a term we used to describe our head-strong daughters) — and confidence. Her presidency with the Junior League of Edmonton was quite remarkable. She ran political campaigns for other candidates, then went on to run as a candidate in a municipal election. Nicole is a born leader and a 'do-er.'

After our first year of university, I took a full-time job outside of Sherwood Park and lived with my grandmother for the summer. I eventually had a boyfriend and became pregnant a few months later. It was an incredibly stressful time for me and my family. When I told my parents, Nicole stayed with me that evening as I sobbed and tried to process it all. Nicole was so supportive and helpful at that time, as one of her superpowers is 'listening for greatness.' In 1984, I had my baby, got married a few months later, and moved to Athabasca, Alta.

I lived in Athabasca for a few years. I hated it there mostly because it was a remote small town, and I had no family there. I focused on raising my family as I had my three kids by 1989, all before I turned 25. Nicole and I didn't talk or see much of each other for a few years. She was busy at school, travelling and developing a relationship with her soon-to-be husband. It was during this time that we drifted apart because my life then was so completely different than hers.

Still, when I had my third child, I asked Nicole and Gavin to be his godparents and I in turn was asked to be the godmother to Nicole's first child. That was very special for both of us.

Nicole and Gavin got married in 1988 at a beautiful ceremony and then lived in Edmonton. Nicole was finishing school and then started her family, and I still lived in Athabasca, so once again we didn't see each other much for a few years.

In 1990, I moved back to Sherwood Park, which to me felt like returning to civilization — I was so happy to be back. Nicole and I would get together for our 'stitch-and-bitch' sessions, where we would do needlework (cross-stitching) at one of our homes. A piece that Nicole stitched for me is hanging on the wall upstairs and I think of her every time I walk by it. I laugh now when I think about those evenings as they were so much fun — we talked about everything and reminisced about the years before we had children. Sometimes Mamma Guay would join us, which was also great. We worked through our problems and challenges and shared the good things that were happening in our lives. We stayed up way too late as there was always so much to talk about. It was truly wonderful.

My family moved to Calgary in 1997. It was a difficult move for me. Nicole was extremely helpful, encouraging me to pursue my current career as a tax accountant. In return, I was able to help Nicole with her accounting class when she worked on her MBA several years ago. However, it soon became quite apparent that accounting was not Nicole's strongest skill, not one of her superpowers.

My brain works well in an analytical, logical and critical thinking environment and wraps very well around numbers. That and my attention to detail and organizational skills are my superpowers (and great qualities for a tax accountant). When Nicole and I are having a conversation, she sometimes says: "Monica, you are losing me in all the details." Nicole's brain is more empathetic and compassionate; she has a warm personality and is so thoughtful. These traits, along with her fierce determination, are how she excels in her career and life in general. Nicole and I have always respected our gifts, and we have challenged one another.

In the almost 50 years that we have confided in each other, I don't ever recall us fighting about anything or having a period in our lives where we were not speaking because we were angry. We have always had mutual respect, and we share many of the same qualities. Nicole and I have always been ambitious, determined and kind, and we understand the importance of family, career and responsibility.

Nicole became ill a few years ago, underwent surgery and needed time to recover. We talked on the phone, and I listened to her as she processed what was happening to her. She came through it all, thankfully. I do recall wondering what my life would have been like without her (I shudder to think) and was so grateful that she got through it.

In the last few years, I have leaned on Nicole many times. My mother became ill in early 2019 and I travelled back and forth from Calgary to Sherwood Park to visit, help care for her, and support my dad. Nicole checked on me often and at the very end, came by with dinner for my family. This was during COVID and my life seemed to be spinning out of control. Nicole helped keep me moving forward.

That period was also very challenging as it was the beginning of the end of my marriage. The last few years I have certainly been at my most vulnerable. Nicole provided grounding. Most importantly, she reminded me that I deserve to be happy. As one of the first people I talked to about this big life-changing decision, she was 100-per-cent supportive. And in her caring, direct way, she said: "Who cares about what anybody thinks? You need to do what will make you happy." I have recently been able to come to terms with some issues and vowed to (and have) been able to move forward. Nicole has been so influential in steering me on this new life path, and shares my excitement about my future plans.

I look forward to many more years of spending time with Nicole. We both love to talk about our careers, travel and family — especially our children and grandchildren. We never have and never will run out of things to talk about and share. The amazing thing about a lifelong friendship is that even if you don't talk to one another for awhile, you can always pick up where you left off.

Now that we are turning 60, we can both sit back and be proud of the work we did as mothers, because our children are doing very well in life. Over the next few years, hopefully we should be slowing down in our careers. Perhaps we could travel together and maybe even resurrect our evenings of 'stitch and bitch' from 30 years ago. But now, with my failing eyesight, I can't do needlework anymore and in any case, it is not so practical. I am happy to knit (as I find knitting incredibly therapeutic) all evening and will teach her if she wants to learn. We would have to rename the evening 'knit and split' because as we get older, we will split a gut laughing!

Monica Blackmore

I am lucky to have three wonderful children, a son-in-law, and am a grandmother (Baba – as we are Ukrainian) to the two most beautiful little boys who steal my heart.

After a career working with textiles, and finding myself in Calgary, I went back to school and have grown to love my heartwork as a tax accountant for the last 27 years.

As an avid, avid gardener, and having spent my lifetime loving to sew and do crafts, my latest love is knitting, which my family and close friends might say is an addiction.

I have met so many incredible people and made amazing friends in my journey. My oldest friend, the author of this anthology, has been my "bestie" and closest friend for almost 50 years. Being a part of this anthology and reflecting on my friendships has been an invaluable experience.

Cherished Memories:
Timeless Moments Shared Together

Darlene O'Keefe

This chapter starts with two little girls who had just moved to Sherwood Park in the summer of 1973. I had moved with my family from Saskatoon and Nicole had relocated with hers from Winnipeg. Our school year started at Jean Vanier School, which had just opened. The floors weren't even finished when we started classes, but a new school was exciting.

We were both in Grade 4 in Sister Herle's class. She was very strict and had big, brown, intense owl eyes. I remember being afraid of her, but since Nicole and I didn't talk back and did our work, we never had her pointing stick banged on our desks.

My friend had a superpower: she spoke French! This was very cool to me. At the end of Grade 4, she moved to a new school that opened in her subdivision, so I didn't reconnect with her until I went to that school for Grades 7 and 8.

Monica was the third member of our friend trio, and the three of us took part in many exciting activities together. There were many sleepovers, soccer, school plays, band concerts, swimming, and bike rides. When we went to Nicole's house, her dad Andy would play the piano, and Jacko, their cute pup, would sing for us. Her little brothers Chris and Bobby were always around and were very sweet. Louise, her mom, was one of the girls. We spent lots of time chatting with her.

When we went to Grade 9, the real fun began. Band, choir, handbells, soccer, swimming, and roller-skating on the weekends. There were trips to Daysland and Jasper, where we quite possibly applied more mascara than had ever been worn. (We missed out on the fake lash era but would have loved them.) There were golf course parties, birthday parties at a place we called Birthday Road, and car rides with older boys we shouldn't have gone out with.

Monica, Nicole, and I decided to play field hockey in Grade 9 and joined a team in Ardrossan, a nearby town. We got to play in the Alberta Summer Games and spend a night sleeping (but I don't think we slept) on a gym floor in St. Albert. That was also the year we tried smoking. Enough about that — it was a bad idea and very short-lived.

My 16th birthday gift from my parents was a trip to Manitoba to stay with Nicole and her family at their cabin on Lake Winnipeg. I flew to Winnipeg and Nicole and Andy picked me up at the airport. Monica came later. We decided one Saturday night at the lake that we would stay up for the sunrise. However, in Nicole's family, Sunday morning meant church and Louise and Andy didn't care how late we had stayed up — we were going to mass. We slept the rest of the day because we could hardly keep our eyes open in church. (Now I am officially a sunset person because it doesn't require me to stay up late or get up early.)

During our stay, we went to a nearby beach called Victoria Beach, which had an old carousel where we met three Italian brothers (one for each of us!) That could have spelled trouble but our time at the beach was limited. Andy came back to get us just as he promised, and we didn't see the brothers again.

I also remember some kitchen adventures with Nicole. One time, when I was having a sleepover at Nicole's place, we decided to make pizza. Out came the Kraft pizza box and we used every type of cheese and all of the sandwich meat in the fridge. I think it weighed about 25 pounds. Andy wasn't too impressed with us. We also decided it was time to drink coffee so we made a whole pot, then promptly decided after one sip that it wasn't for us. Only later in life would we learn that coffee is the true elixir of life. We had so many fun times together and I can't think of a better person to make memories with.

Author Ally Condie wrote in her book Matched: "Growing apart doesn't change the fact that for a long time we grew side by side; our roots will always be tangled." That describes what happened with Nicole and me. We both changed schools for Grade 12 and that was a turning point in our relationship.

Life was busy and we went our separate ways, only occasionally spending time together. I got pregnant with my first son the summer after Grade 12 and, in retrospect, I pulled away from all my friends, knowing that my life had changed course. The next seven years were spent as a single parent going to university and raising my son Justin. I ignored my friendships through this period and I'm honestly not sure why except that life was pretty overwhelming.

Over the next few years, all of our friends seemed to get married, which gave me the opportunity to reconnect. Nicole and Gavin also got married during that period. I hadn't had the opportunity to get to know Gavin, but I could see how happy Nicole was, so I knew they were a perfect fit. If you know Nicole, you know that on most days, she will likely be wearing something she has eaten on her shirt. Monica decided that wasn't going to happen on Nicole's big day, so she sewed Nicole a bib to wear during their wedding dinner. Nicole has a fantastic sense of humour so of course she wore it!

Nicole travelled to Idaho where I was doing my Master's in Speech Pathology in early 1989. She was sick but I managed to drug her with liquid cough syrup (even though she gags on liquid medicine). I don't remember exactly what we did that weekend, but I do remember how much I appreciated that visit when I was so far away from home. She was an incredible friend to come all that way to visit Justin and I loved her for it.

After university, I moved to Medicine Hat to start my career, got married and had two more sons. Life was busy, to say the least. Trips back to Sherwood Park were always about family and I rarely had time to see friends. I do remember coming with my two youngest boys to visit Nicole and meet her girls, Sarah and Lauren, when they were little, but that was a rare event. I would mostly hear about what she was doing through my parents, who often ran into her at the grocery store or at church.

Fast forward to 2021 and I was doing contract work as a speech pathologist in a Northern Alberta First Nations community. A new psychologist by the name of Sarah was also coming there to work. I knew at once that she had to be Nicole and Gavin's Sarah. I couldn't wait to get to know her as I hadn't seen her since she was about five or six years old. The moment I laid eyes on her, it was like seeing someone I had known forever. She is the best possible combination of Gavin and Nicole, and one of the kindest and sweetest people I have ever met, a true gem. We had many laughs when I told her some of the stories about her mom and me growing up. On one of our trips up north, we Facetimed Grandma Louise, who I hadn't seen for years. It was so incredible to talk with her. I hope I can see her in person someday soon and give her a big hug.

I have had many friendships over the years and I cherish all of them. Many people seem to have patterns in their friendships, and I guess I do too. Most of my friends are people I have known for many years, gathering them from various life experiences.

My longest friendship is with Bev, who I met in Grade 1. We were inseparable for those first three years and then my family moved to Sherwood Park. We spent weeks at a time every summer between our homes, and wrote letters and phoned each other in between those summer visits. After university, she moved to Lethbridge and we moved to Medicine Hat. Work, marriages and motherhood kept us both busy, so although we had visits in those years, they didn't happen often. I rarely see her now but when we do connect, it's like we haven't been apart. A true friend knows the real you and you can just carry on from where you left off.

Another of my incredible friends is Penny. We went to university together in Idaho for two years. She has a daughter, a year older than Justin, so the kids are a part of our friendship. They went to daycare and school together while we went to university. Although we now live thousands of miles apart, we have some crazy and wonderful memories together. She is insanely beautiful both inside and out and has a kind and compassionate soul. She is my ride-or-die and if I ever need help, she would be the one I reach out to. She is another friend with whom time stands still. A true friend knows the real you and there is honesty, loyalty, and respect in the relationship. Friends don't judge and they are good listeners.

I love having reconnected with Nicole through Sarah and feel incredibly honoured that she asked me to write a chapter in this anthology. I look forward to many more happy times together with a dear friend. I love you, Nicole.

Darlene O'Keefe

Life is such a crazy ride! I don't often get to reflect on myself so thank you for this opportunity, Nicole. I'm a mom of three adult sons, a grandma to a beautiful granddaughter and two sweet guys. My husband Matt and I have been married for 34 years.

I have spent my career working with children and I would describe myself as a "Champion for Children." I am a speech/language pathologist passionate about helping children become their best selves. Children are my jam! I credit my family for supporting my career dreams. My work has taken me to many interesting places and presented many opportunities.

A friend is someone with whom you have established a unique connection. There is love and respect that is constant as it was solidified early on. Nicole and I have had many seasons together but sadly also missed many. I sincerely hope we have more in the future.

Reconnecting with A Sunflower's Radiance

Monica Kryska

As I reflect on friendship and the many connections that it brings, I am most aware of the many who have been and still are in my life and others who have passed through my life.

Nicole is one of those friends with whom I have many connections. Even though we don't see each other often, she is the one who reconnects with me, and for that, I am grateful. I look to her as an example of someone who is not afraid to reach out, even when time has passed. For my part, I am usually afraid of being seen as neglectful of our friendship, since time has passed and we no longer have reliable methods of connecting, like work or volunteering.

I met Nicole through Girl Guides when her daughter was in my unit, and she volunteered to step into leadership with me. We had many laughs and worked really well together. A federal election gave us the opportunity to develop a Girl Guide meeting where she and I role-played as prime minister and leader of the opposition in a leaders' debate. To keep it non-partisan, we mixed up the names of the real politicians. (I think we were Stephen Martin and Paul Harper!)

Guiding connected three things that were common ground in our friendship: leadership, outdoor camping and community service.

We did a lot of camping with our Guides. Some of our themes included Camp Canada over the July 1 weekend; Camp Tekakwitha (where we learned about Indigenous cultures, met elders and participated in circle dancing); and a Harry Potter Camp, with an environmental theme based on our four houses of water, air, fire and Earth. Nicole gave it her all and embraced whatever came her way. Her Guiding name was Sunflower and it was perfect. Truly, she brought her bright and lively spirit to all our activities. Through our Guiding connection, I learned to trust in us as a team, to not take myself so seriously, and to rest and enjoy the process no matter the outcome. I am still practising these life lessons!

The best of our camps was the Harry Potter theme. Our Guides were at the perfect age and avid readers of the series. Planning this camp showcased the creativity that Nicole and I shared as leaders. We had so much fun creating and co-ordinating the activities, and our goal of an amazing weekend camp experience came to fruition.

Our camp started with a hat-sorting event in the great hall. Owl deliveries arrived each morning with the schedule for the day (a magical experience for one of our Guides, who really believed the owl had come during the night). There was also a potions class where we made some wicked, but healthy smoothies, and a wand-making class. On our final evening, each house put on an amazing show of creative, entertaining and memorable magical wizardry. Unbeknownst to them, this built their leadership presentation skills.

Over the years, Nicole has always had a keen interest in governance and politics and has worked to bring integrity and openness to the electoral process. She is keenly interested in encouraging others to get involved in the political process and is a stalwart defender of democracy. I played a small part in helping her during the huge process of running as a candidate in a municipal election. She spent summers door-knocking all over Sherwood Park to connect with voters. She used those moments to listen to concerns and I saw her truly connect with people. She easily and naturally creates the moments of connection that build faith and trust.

Some years ago, Nicole reached out to ask if I would be a 'babysitter' for her. She had been scheduled for very delicate but necessary brain surgery and could not be left alone for some weeks after the procedure.

She had gathered her village of friends and slotted them in for time periods to assist her at home while she recovered. It was an honour to be invited to share this time with her. I have always admired Nicole's gift of vulnerability when she needs help, and she honours her friends by inviting them along on her journey. There was not much she needed except presence. What a gift for me: another space of connection.

We also connect in our faith lives. We are both practising Catholics and active in our faith community at Our Lady of Perpetual Help Parish. Together with our husbands, we are involved in peer-support marriage ministries to help build healthy marriages (Worldwide Marriage Encounter) and support couples who are struggling in their marriages (Retrouvaille Marriage Help program). Both of these ministries support couples through the sharing of our own marriage journeys. One of the premises of both these programs is the strength we gain by sharing ourselves within a safe and caring community. Friendships formed within our respective ministries span decades. These are true spaces of deep connection and friendship.

To Nicole, thank you for many years of connection and friendship. You have taught me much about courage, resilience, perseverance and trust. God bless you now and always, my friend!

Monica Kryska

I am a wife, mother of four, mother-in-law of three, grandmother of two. Brian and I have been married for 37 years. I am a lifelong Catholic, born in Ottawa to my U.K. parents, and an Albertan for over 42 years. I graduated from Queen's University in Kingston in 1981 and University of Alberta in 1985 in occupational therapy. I have been an OT, stay-at-home mom and lifelong volunteer. I have volunteered in student governments, OT professional organizations, La Leche League, Girl Guides, Retrouvaille, Vacation Bible Camp, BOG St. Joe's College, and have had many roles in my faith community.

I value faith, joy, truth, beauty, goodness and connection. I appreciate deep conversations, excellent books, art, long walks, friendship, travel, camping, quiet reflection, and the interrelatedness of everything: God's perfection is in everything from the universe to the subatomic particle. Currently I enjoy faith-related podcasts and am revisiting Father Brown on BritBox.

A Perspective

Maureen Landry

When I was young, what attracted me to my friends was proximity. If I could see you, you would be my friend. I wasn't allowed to wander around neighbourhoods or go to playgrounds by myself looking for kids to be my friends – so I needed them to be next door, or down the street. Beyond that, if you had a happy-go-lucky nature, I would like you. If you were curious and engaged in life, that was good too. It was almost like I could be friends with anyone who happened to be nearby.

But adult life – and real friendships-don't work that way. Adult friendships don't happen instantaneously, like they did in childhood. When you are an adult, you need to seek out friends who bring meaning to your life. You need to cultivate those friendships, and you have to keep working at them. Now, I am attracted to people who accept me for who I am and who I accept wholeheartedly, or who were somehow sent to me to teach a life lesson that I have asked to learn.

These are the people who shaped me, the ones who make up my friendship tapestry:

My first friend was born Jan.1 and I was born on the 21st. We were neighbours and friends for the first five years of my life. But when I moved away, we didn't keep in touch (hard to do when you're five years old).

When we moved back to the neighbourhood a few years later, I hung out with the same group of kids, we reconnected and he became a life-long friend. He was one of my grad dates. I still have love and affinity for him, even though I rarely see him. He's in my heart. Did I take care of him or did he take care of me? I think it was mutual — we looked out for each other. Maybe we still do in some ways.

I moved for Grade 1 to a smaller town and there were a lot of girls my age. Probably about 10 and I was riding high on life, having so many friend possibilities. I am still friends with one of those girls. What initially attracted me to her? In a nutshell, she was everything I wanted to be. She was a girlie girl and I was a tomboy. She was fashionable (so was her mother) and she had Barbies. She had passions — fashion and decorating — and a way of seeing the world that I wanted a piece of. She was creative and present in whatever she was involved in. I saw myself as plain and simple.

My Grade 1 picture is me in a dress with a white collar and a tie that looks like a girl's version of a necktie. I did not normally wear dresses. I remember playing on the swing on picture day and falling in the mud and getting my dress all dirty. My friend showed up in a yellow dress (mine was snot green) with her hair nicely curled in pigtails with a matching choker necklace. For that Grade 1 picture, my hair was a fetching bowl cut. We are very different but still good friends. She says she can always talk to me about anything.

What attracted me to my next best friend? Being there for me. I had moved back to our old city in Grade 5 and everyone else already had friends. Luckily, she became mine. We explored adolescence and high school together. I was a people-pleaser and a butt-kisser and she graciously allowed me to be that way. She also allowed me to be tough, strong and a leader. She quietly supported me. She also told me I was a source of support for her as well. We had lots of adventurous and fun times. She certainly taught me how to laugh. Laugh at life and most importantly, laugh at myself. We stuck close together through high school and had other friends, but she was my best friend then.

This same friend and I moved to Banff after high school to live and work for a year, with jobs at a hotel and rooms in staff accommodation. The day we started work as chambermaids, my mom phoned the hotel to ask if we had been hired to be prostitutes! My friend was there with me through that embarrassment. I recently spent a couple days hanging out with her, my husband Gerry and my sister Joan. We had some relaxing times and some great laughs – and we shared lots of love.

I started university in Saskatoon after that Banff year. Those were three long years because I never made any good friends at school. But I interacted with lots of cool people and learned lots — not from school but from campus life. In the summers, I worked in Kananaskis Country and met some awesome people, including the young woman who would become my next best friend. We were roommates in Château Atco and quickly became fast friends, because we were both from Saskatchewan. We had some wild crazy adventures in life and in nature. We cleaned outhouses with finesse! She was at my wedding and we are still friends today. She is such a gentle, sweet soul. An extremely smart lady who is so down-to-earth. She can pick up with you in a moment like it was yesterday.

My next best friend took me hiking in the backcountry and showed me how to handle myself in those situations, physically and mentally. We shared a lot and faced a lot of challenges together. I learned how to trust my physical instincts and my emotional acumen. I am grateful for our intense short-term relationship. When I saw her 10 months ago, there was a palpable excitement and connection on both our parts. Those were some heady times of my life. Kananaskis Country was a haven in a crazy world.

I was introduced to my next best friend by a mutual friend at a bar. He was a pleasant-looking, fun, easy-going guy. We danced a bit, then he asked me to slow dance and held me close. If I am honest, it felt weird and comforting at the same time. He certainly left an impression on me. Over the years, I would see him at parties, cabarets and bars. Always happy-go-lucky, down-to-earth and genuine. He always made me feel heard. Always good for some great conversations, laughter and dancing. I married him in 1989.

And now to Nicole, the creator of this wonderful anthology about friendship, and another of my best friends. I met her through our kids, who attended the same school. Here was another professional mom with similar interests and with whom I could have some intelligent, meaningful, fun conversations. She was confident, fun and connected to those around her and beyond. This is how I wanted to show up in the world. We had some fun competitions in the class to see who could perform the teacher-assigned duties quicker or more efficiently. Always with a sense of fun.

Nicole and I shared a passion for showing up for the world. I was a Girl Guide Sparks leader one year and one of her daughters attended, along with my daughter. Nicole was a great source of help and inspiration as we navigated creative ways for the girls to grasp an understanding of how the world works and develop skills for their future. The next year we were co-leaders in Brownies. We got out to lots of community activities and camps. We had a great year together and Nicole completed beautiful picture memory books for the girls.

Some years later, Nicole asked me to assist her in her run for municipal politics. I went door-to-door with her and called constituents. I was challenged and blessed to have an opportunity to connect with people and learn how to listen. Connecting people is a passion Nicole and I share. I've always admired Nicole's aspirations and dreams about how the world could be and am always challenged and pleased to share those spaces with her.

Nicole's superpower is developing and sustaining deep and meaningful friendships, and I am grateful that she includes me in her village of friends.

When I think of my adult friendships like the one with Nicole, I understand the qualities that attract me to people. I am attracted to beautiful people – and I don't mean physically beautiful. I mean people with a joie-de-vivre, a beautiful heart (of love and acceptance) and peaceful souls, or at least souls that are my level of peace or higher. I am attracted to people whose faces light up when they see me; their voices raise in a little lilt when they first greet me. I hope that's how I show up for them.

I am attracted to people who are up to something in life. People who want to be of service to others, who want to make the world a better place. I can hear it in their voice, the words they speak and I see it in the gleam in their eyes.

How do you cultivate lasting friendships with people? You attune to it. You listen for it, you speak to it, you show up in your actions and behaviours. You call forth a lasting friendship with them and in doing so in yourself and together you call it forward for the rest of the world.

"Our deepest fear is not that we are inadequate. Our deepest fear is that we are powerful beyond measure. It is our light, not our darkness that most frightens us. We ask ourselves, 'Who am I to be brilliant, gorgeous, talented, fabulous?' Actually, who are you not to be? You are a child of God. Your playing small does not serve the world. There is nothing enlightened about shrinking so that other people won't feel insecure around you. We are all meant to shine, as children do. We were born to make manifest the glory of God that is within us. It's not just in some of us; it's in everyone. And as we let our own light shine, we unconsciously give other people permission to do the same. As we are liberated from our own fear, our presence automatically liberates others."— Marianne Williamson, A Return to Love: Reflections on the Principles of A Course in Miracles.

Maureen Landry

https://www.facebook.com/profile.php?id=100000943365508

Hello....my name is Maureen. I am a human being blah, blah, blah. Life is a roller-coaster ride. Sometimes it's euphoric, challenging, inspiring, scary, surreal, and 15 other adjectives but it's always an adventure.

My ride is always full of people, friends, family, my spouse and acquaintances. I sometimes choose not to see or feel their presence, but they are always there. I just need to reach out. Some have been on this ride with me for eons, some for fun or to impart some wisdom on me. I learn to appreciate them all.

True meaning in life is found in service to others. Let your friendship story be so inspired.

From Russia to Canada with Love

Nadia Zotova

Note: Nadia speaks Russian, Dari and English, but writing in English doesn't come easily to her. She sat down with one of our project's writing coaches to share her story.

I understand you were born in Russia. What was your life like there?

I grew up in a town called Maloyaroslavets, which is not too far from Moscow. It was a small place, where everybody knew everybody. We lived on a farm.

Then, I moved to Moscow when I was a teenager and lived in an apartment that belonged to my grandmother. I met my husband Dawood there — he was my neighbour. He was a salesman. I worked in a daycare centre.

Why did you decide to move to Canada?

My husband was from Afghanistan and it was hard for him because he didn't have papers to stay in Russia. So we decided to go to Canada or the United States — whichever would accept us first. We came to Canada in 2006, with our two-year-old son, Dima.

We went to London, Ontario, where my husband had some family.

Was it difficult at first?

It was a very hard adjustment. Everything was different and I missed my friends and family. At first, it was hard for him to find work — his first job was delivering pizza flyers. Later he got work as a house painter.

I was taking ESL classes but I was pregnant with my next child and it was hard to continue.

Learning English was hard. I remember so many funny stories that happened because of miscommunication.

You were in London for nine years, then you moved to Edmonton. Why did you move?

There wasn't much work for my husband in London, or for me. And we wanted to try a new place. He had a friend in Edmonton who introduced him to the city and helped him find a job. He moved in 2014 and I followed with the children the next year. By then, we had three kids — the girls are Deanna and Anna.

You started working as a house cleaner in 2016. Why did you choose that line of work?

Cleaning was a good job for my situation. I wanted a job that would be flexible, to allow me to concentrate on my children. It's especially important now because they are teenagers (19, 17 and 15) and I want to be around for them. They are my priority.

How did you meet Nicole?

I haven't known her that long, less than a year. I met her through her friend Kim. I was cleaning for Kim.

I really liked Nicole right away. She is very nice, she is calm, she's kind and she has been a big supporter. And she's a really good listener.

What do you talk about?

I can talk to her about anything. I share some of my problems and she helps me figure out some solutions. We talk about marriage and raising daughters — she has two wonderful grown daughters.

She is very honest — I like that. I don't like people who go behind your back. I like people who tell it straight. She is older than me, and more of a professional person, so for me, it's wonderful that I can go to her for advice.

She helped my daughter Deanna prepare for her first job interview and she got the job! She's been a beautiful support to me and my kids. She's helping me make sure they become professionals and good people.

What makes Nicole a good friend?

Nicole is always so friendly — she's always hugging me. I have a lot to learn from her. Especially about exercise and looking after yourself. She's always out there walking, jogging, being active. For Nicole, there are no excuses for not getting out there. I need to do more of that.

What about other friends?

I was an only child, so when I was growing up, I had to find playmates. In Russia, my two best friends were girls I met in daycare and we were friends through Grade 11. Victoria and Julia. We know each other like sisters. We trust and support each other.

We're still friends. Even though we are far apart, we still talk on WhatsApp about three times a month. It's important to keep up these old friendships. It's important to make that effort. They love to ask me about my life in Canada.

Why are friendships so important?

We all need support, especially if we're in a new country. Now that my children are teenagers and young adults, and they don't need as much of my help, I'm making more time to go out with friends, have them over for lunch or go for walks.

Nadia Zotova

I am a mother of two teenagers and a young adult. My husband and I immigrated to Canada with the dream of pursuing better opportunities for our family. We have embraced our new life here while staying true to our roots. I take pride in my Russian and he in his Dari heritage. We have worked hard to keep our cultural traditions alive through language, traditional food, and sharing stories from our homelands.

Professionally, I own and operate a housecleaning business, which I find fulfilling and fun. The physical nature of my work allows me to stay active and healthy, almost like getting paid to exercise every day. Over the years, my business has introduced me to wonderful clients, some of whom have become friends. After work, I enjoy sharing BBQs, dinners and activities centred around food and wine with these new friends, further enriching my life here in Canada.

You Contain Multitudes: Calling on Your Masculine and Feminine Qualities to Deepen Friendships

Rie Algeo Gilsdorf

In high school, I had many guy friends, some black friends, and one friend who was always the 'black Guy'. As in, his surname was Guy. He was one of the handful of black and Latino students who had been recruited to our high school as part of a wave of racial and gender integration of private schools in the 1970s in the United States.

Mail call/Male call? Blending in, with my denim jacket, long, straight hair and no makeup, circa 1974

I was also part of the integration wave as a pioneering female student at our formerly all-boys' high school in my small California town. It remained a boarding school for the boys. The girls were day students who went home each evening, and we were all white. Outnumbered four-to-one by the boys, we stuck together to navigate how much to assimilate and how much to just be who we were: girls. The black and

Latino boys also hung out together in a group they informally called 'the family.' At the time I didn't know much about cultural assimilation and it didn't occur to me that for different aspects of our developing identities, both groups were going through similar challenges.

The four-to-one ratio of boys to girls gave rise to many things. First, there was a masculine ethos to the place that we all adopted. It was a remnant of the founder's British boys' boarding school experience. We were called by our last names (think of Hogwarts professors spitting out the names Potter or Malfoy). All of our academic subjects were taught by men. We took a certain pride in roughing it that extended from the formal outdoor education program to the remodelled chicken coops that served as classrooms, to tolerance of the earwigs found in every door jamb. These squirmy, pincered bugs became our school mascot while I was there, as much to set ourselves apart from the more highbrow schools as to gross out their girly cheerleaders.

The steep boy-girl ratio also imprinted my relationships with males. For the first few months, I was as boy-crazy as any straight teenage girl. Then I realized that I couldn't possibly have a crush on all the cute guys, much less date them. This led to me developing an important skill: how to be friends with boys and later, men. Looking back, the ingredients are:

- Projecting unflappability, especially when someone is trying to gross you out or prank you. Better yet, act like you're part of the joke until you can flip it on them. Once at a dance, a guy I was dancing with kept turning his back on me to face his buddies. I could tell he was making faces because they were cracking up. I took advantage of his looking away to peek out from behind him and make faces of my own. He eventually figured it out and conceded defeat. I never had that problem again.

- Not shying away from stating your own case, debating or disagreeing. Say it like you mean it. I figured out in the classroom that guys would often state an answer with a bravado that seemed like 100-per-cent certainty — but that I knew was wrong. This was a window into confidence as a style they adopted more than as an actual feeling. I learned to put aside a little of my feminine perfectionism and enter the conversation projecting confidence, if not full-on bravado. I'm still better at this in the classroom or professional settings than socially.
- Not objectifying them by projecting Prince Charming fantasies on them. Projections can lead to flirtatious fun, but they can also make you lose sight of the friend they are being in the present moment — or the friend you could be by listening to them. And if you don't want to be objectified, start by not objectifying them. It sets your expectations and your tone. If you want to be friends, be friends. If you want to flirt with Prince Charming, do that. Just don't mix the two up.

Of all these boys, Guy stood out as a natural leader. In his group of friends, he was always looking out for younger boys of colour and helping them acclimate to the school so that they could realize their potential there. He served with me in student government. By his senior year, his leadership extended to being president of the entire student body. He was a little older, a sharp dresser and incredibly cool. He brought music from Los Angeles back after each school break, music that wouldn't play on our rural radio stations for months. And, like me, Guy steered clear of the drug culture of the times in order to be serious about academics.

Now, in other circumstances, I might have developed a crush on Guy. Instead, he and I became friends, part of a group that often gathered to make pizza from scratch in my mom's kitchen, or learn the latest L.A. dance craze at a school party (I vividly remember Guy teaching us the

Bump), or attend the weddings of our older brothers and sisters. Guy and I, along with both of our moms, sat together as the only non-Latino guests at one of these weddings, a traditional Mexican-Catholic ceremony. Once again, we found ourselves on equal footing, helping each other understand and appreciate the cultural phenomenon we were experiencing.

After high school, we all went off to college. Having been raised in a small town, I couldn't wait to get to the big city. Having been raised in the city, Guy appreciated small-town life. He ended up moving back to that small town when it was time to raise a family, shortly after I left it for good. But that ensured that I would see him on and off throughout the years when I came home to visit. In a quirk of fate, we ended up being present for the interment of both of our mothers' ashes. We became the comforting someone who 'knew each other when.' Someone who could tell stories about my mom handing him a lump of pizza dough and asking him to toss it, with complete confidence that he'd be able to; or about his mom always being simultaneously the most elegant and the most down-to-earth person in any room. By retelling those small moments, we served as mirrors that helped each other reframe the patterns of our parents' lives to see deeper meanings.

These memories weren't only meaningful to me. At my mother's wake, my teenage son heard them. They fleshed out his picture of his grandmother and how she impacted another teenage boy all those years ago. As we lowered Guy's mom's ashes into a church courtyard, his daughter was there to hear my stories of her grandmother. It was another layer of bonding for our families.

The current chapter of my friendship with Guy began when we ran into each other at a reunion and found that we were both working on equity projects. Guy was entering a new term on the school's Board of Trustees and had been appointed the chair of the Diversity, Equity & Inclusion (DEI) committee. He joked that he'd actually been doing this work for 40 years, since his student days. I was just embarking on my own business venture as a DEI consultant. Guy saw that, collaboratively, we could position ourselves to do some remarkable work with the school that had brought us together. Our perspectives would bring a unique strength and synergy as Guy recounted his experiences as one of the first black boarding students, and I recounted mine as one of the first girl day students.

Guy reintroduced me to his daughter, Cianna, also an alum of the school, who was beginning to make her way into the DEI consulting world. As we worked together to steer the school through the aftermath of George Floyd's death, Cianna and I became friends and colleagues beyond this project. Meanwhile, Guy always had our backs with the board, reminding them whenever they leaned toward settling for the status quo, that we were not just there as alumnae but as DEI experts.

What I've learned from all this is that a true and longstanding friendship integrates elements of the masculine and the feminine. Learning from boys how to state my case and not objectify the other person translates to showing up as myself and allowing the other person to do so as well. These have been important qualities in friendships and business relationships alike. And, it was our ability to be present and vulnerable, two characteristics commonly classified as feminine, that later deepened and strengthened our friendship.

I've also come to appreciate how a true friend can let you grow. When Guy and I met, I was only 13, an insular white kid from a rural town. Guy was one of the first black people I'd ever met. I had no idea his experience would be any different from mine. In the years since, I've developed a more sophisticated understanding of race and culture. I'm grateful that I now can be supportive in a way I never could have back then, and that Guy was able to look past the silly teen he first knew to the collaborator he saw I could be.

Of course, I wasn't thinking systemically about masculine and feminine friendship dynamics as a teenager. That's something I've been reflecting on since recently taking a course on feminine power. The course was where I met Nicole, who I could tell was going to be a great collaborator from the way she showed up in the online group. She lived up to the potential of a supportive community by both posting her thoughts, questions and experiences as well as responding supportively and honestly to others. When the course ended, we decided to become 'power partners,' to support, amplify and be accountable to one another. In this process, Nicole has shown me how actively encouraging your partner to grow can jump-start a friendship.

At one of our first meetings, I was telling Nicole a story of my upbringing that I thought was just background. But she immediately caught something I had not. She noticed big cultural contrasts throughout my childhood, moving back and forth between public and private school, which prepared me for the equity-focused career I have today. This witnessing, mirroring and naming is so important to illuminate the blind spots we all have, the things we cannot see about ourselves. In turning the beam of attention to my blind spots, she gently nudged me in a growth direction.

Many of my best clients have been people of colour who have grown up in proximity to whiteness, light-skinned or white-presenting folks, biracial people with one white parent or Indigenous Peoples who have grown up in a white suburb, etc. Hearing that, Nicole envisioned a specific niche for me as a coach, where I could put to work my lived experience of navigating between cultures. Her vision opened my imagination to new possibilities — another nudge toward growth. Because, though it was tantalizing, this niche was a bit of a stretch for me to envision. I had internalized so many messages about staying in my lane as a white woman that I defined my ideal client as a woman much like me — white, middle-aged, middle-class. I went on with my work without really investigating the idea.

The next time we met, she asked what had happened to the idea, and she coined a really interesting term: 'culture broker.' That term crystallized something for me, a new frame of reference that I get to define. The lane that I stay in doesn't have to be some old, stale concept that others have put on me. I can stay in my lane by creating an entirely new lane. This opened up an imaginative space that gave me enough emotional cover to re-examine the limiting beliefs I was carrying and begin to let them go. Her persistence in asking me what had happened with the idea, rather than politely letting it slide, held me accountable to myself in a non-judgmental way. This was the final encouragement I needed to truly grow.

We all need people to mirror back to us the patterns of our lives, amplify our capacity to imagine our futures and hold space for generative dialogue until we can grow into that future version of ourselves. This level of honesty, presence and vision is something rarely seen outside of long-term friendships or close family relationships. It incorporates both traditionally masculine witnessing and forthrightness along with typically feminine mirroring and encouragement. In both my lengthy association with Guy and my relatively brief one with Nicole, accessing our whole selves has deepened the relationship from peers to trusted friends.

Rie Algeo Gilsdorf

Embody Equity
Facilitator & Founder

https://www.linkedin.com/in/riegilsdorf/
https://www.facebook.com/groups/164798725481730
https://www.instagram.com/embodyequity/
https://www.embodyequity.com

Rie Algeo Gilsdorf (she/her/ella) is passionate about connecting people across cultural distance and racial difference, integrating mind and body, science and art, healing and change-making. With master's degrees in biology and modern dance, Rie organically infuses the perspectives of the body - from the physiology of trauma to the subtlety of gesture - into all her work. Her company, Embody Equity, is dedicated to building a common culture that heals and upholds us all. Knowing that the confluence of cultural streams will always produce turbulence, and then a more powerful river, she teaches, coaches and mediates, helping people navigate this turbulence with confidence, fluency and grace.

Rie recognized a kindred spirit in Nicole van Kuppeveld when they met in a women's centred coaching course and were both noticing connections between empowerment and culture. Rie and Nicole continue as 'power partners' who mirror and amplify each other's greater possibilities.

Close Friends

Ruth HM

The COVID-19 pandemic caused a friendship crisis. How do I know this? There have been a plethora of articles on the topic of friends. Friendship has been analyzed to bits by academic experts, newspaper columnists, social media influencers and anyone who can form an opinion. Now it's my turn!

Suzanne Degges-White, PhD (psychology) says there are seven types of friendship, while Sanjana Gupta, MA (journalism) says there are four. What is a girl to do? How do I decide how many types of friendships there can be? I don't. Instead, I have looked at where the writers intersect and go from there. To add a bit of confusion to my analysis, I will toss in bits and pieces from the New York Times opinion columnist David Brooks. This will be fun because he is opinionated and not an expert, but he quotes experts.

Degges-White and Gupta agree on the categories of close friends and lifelong friends. They lump everyone else into the categories of acquaintances, casual friends, friends of convenience, activity friends and social group friends. Degges-White also has a category called best friends. In some circles, these are known as the sacredly held BFFs. I think that is a millennial acronym. The musician Paul Simon would just call them Al (from his Graceland album).

I'm not curious about the category of lifelong friend. It is easy to understand — they have been around for a long time. We can assume that we like and appreciate these lifelong friends because the relationship has endured. Or they just have so much blackmail material we don't want to endanger ourselves by cutting them off. Close friend: now that title incites questions. What is this thing called a close friend?

How does one make the journey from acquaintance/casual friend to close friend? Is it a fast or slow journey? Do they eventually become the coveted BFF? How important is this close friend?

David Brooks, the *New York Times* opinionated one, quoting some experts, says: "Friendship is transformative." It is a life-altering act. Well, that is a little daunting. Those are big expectations to put on a friendship. How do we know if the friendship is measuring up? Do we keep a little journal? Or do we do an assessment when we have reached our 60th birthday?

Gupta to the rescue! She has taken the term close friend and broken it down into eight definitive characteristics in her article *How the 4 Types of Friendship Fit Into Your Life*. It is easy to evaluate the behaviours of our friends against the eight criteria. Here we go.

Friends provide an emotionally safe place to express yourself.

I found myself newly single in the senior stage of my life. It was time to build some new friendships. How does one embark on such a venture? Well, I decided that the local public library would be a good place to start. Guess who I found? None other than the most famous friend-maker of them all, Dale Carnegie. This is his most famous quote:

> "You can make more friends in two months by becoming interested in other people than you can in two years by trying to get other people interested in you."

I had a plan. I peppered everyone I met with so many questions, they started to get annoyed and if they saw me coming, they would turn in the other direction. One lady on the bus said: "You ask a lot of questions." I gave her my biggest smile.

Carnegie had let me down. I needed a new plan. Enter Marisa G.

Franco, PhD (psychology), a friendship expert. She says that as adults, we have to recreate the infrastructure we had as kids. We can do so by pursuing our favourite hobby in a community. Pursue a hobby in a group and keep showing up.

The keep-showing-up is the hardest part. Spanish lessons were tough. However, I do know how to ask where the bathroom is located and how to offer a friendly hola. Crafting didn't work out either. I kept gluing my fingers together. A friend of a friend of a friend heard of my plight. She offered emotional support and taught me how to play kitchen bridge. As it turns out, the bridge table is a great place for adult women to make new friends. Many bridge courses later, I hang out with a group of exceptional people and we play bridge. The friendships have grown. We now gather socially, go on travel adventures, have interesting discussions and freely share our feelings.

Spending time together is a priority.

Research conducted by Jeffrey Hall, director of the Relationships and Technology Lab at the University of Kansas, found that it takes about 300 hours of togetherness to become close friends. Thankfully this is a lot fewer than the 10,000 hours that author Malcohm Gladwell suggests are needed to master the skills for playing hockey or the cello.

Television personality Oprah Winfrey says if you can survive 11 days, which is approximately 300 hours, in cramped quarters with a friend and come out laughing, your friendship is the real deal.

Time and laughing together are key friendship building ingredients.

These friends know how to provide comfort when you are down.

> "There is nothing like puking with somebody to make you into old friends." —Sylvia Plath (novelist, poet)

Just think of the path you must be travelling on to engage in such a shared experience. You might be travelling on a boat or a train. Then again, it might be a shared virus like the flu or maybe it is a nasty bacterium that caused food poisoning. Or it might be the age-old case of having drunk more than your share of lemon gin. In every circumstance, you and your friend(s) are helping each other. How many times have you held up your friend's hair, so it didn't get yucky? Or consoled their broken heart? You made heartfelt commitments to stay together through thick and thin, or until your parents or some other authority showed up to cart you away.

Comfort can be offered in so many ways and circumstances and creates friendship bonds.

There is always lots of fun and laughter and inside jokes.

How do we define a good friend? It is easy to define a bad friend. My mom was very clear about this. As a young person, I remember that the bad friends were usually the fun friends. Did they become close friends when we didn't get caught and now had secrets and shared experiences to giggle about? When does someone become a close friend? Here are some quotes from unknown authors that might guide us in our decision.

"Friendship must be built on a solid foundation of alcohol, sarcasm, inappropriateness, and shenanigans."

"If you have friends who are as weird as you, then you have everything."

"You don't have to be crazy to be my friend. I'll train you."

"Shenanigans sound like a lot of fun."

Insider jokes are a friend-bonding tool, too. Only people who love dogs, I mean really love dogs, will appreciate this one:

"Good friends discuss their sex lives. Best friends talk about poop."

There was a rescue Labradoodle puppy available for adoption. I had to make the decision quickly. I said yes, signed the papers and we were off. My friend drove the getaway car while I sat in the back with the dog. What's that smell? Oh no, the dog pooped in the car. Undaunted, my friend continued to speed down the highway as I flung dog poop out the window. Her version of this story is much funnier and more graphic. In recounting this story, not everyone had the same level of appreciation for the details.

David Brooks says that we become friends because we delight in each other's company. I must agree. Fun is a key ingredient in developing and maintaining a close friendship.

They are sounding boards and provide feedback and advice.

"A true friend accepts who you are, but also helps you become who you should be."—Anonymous

This quote is positive and encouraging, but don't be fooled. What does "help you become who you should be" really mean? This phrase is kind of like a wolf in sheep's clothing. Have my friends accepted who I am? Heck no! Perish the thought. Friends do not always have the same perspectives as you. However, they usually have the very best intentions for you. For example, when I was younger, one of my friends suggested that I should go to university and use the 'smart' part of 'smart-ass' to get a degree and make something of myself. I thought I was just quick-witted and funny. I am certainly thankful for the lack of acceptance, the feedback, the advice and the push.

They can be counted on. They have our back.

My experience is that reliability, compassion, goodness and a fine sense of humour also contribute to being a close friend. A stuffy-looking educator and author by the name of Laurence J. Peter has come up with a straightforward definition that captures the primary attribute of a close friend who can be counted on.

"You can always tell a real friend: when you've made a fool of yourself s/he doesn't feel you have done a permanent job."

A close friend has many characteristics and attributes but most importantly, has your back and is supportive in the most trying of circumstances.

They will hold you accountable for your actions and decisions.

Let's not be pedantic about this one and just accept that from time to time, your close friend(s) might call you names for some of the choices you make.

The friendship is built on a foundation of love, thoughtfulness and caring.

Michelle Obama in her book Becoming says: "Friendships between women, as many women will tell you, are built of a thousand small kindnesses, swapped back and forth and over again."

Some of those kindnesses involve wine and food. Author Linda Grayson says: "There is nothing better than a friend, unless it is a friend with chocolate." I quite simply agree with her. I really like the chocolates with cherry centres. A close friend can be counted on to bring the right chocolates. They can also be counted on to bring chocolate when you are in need but impaired and not able to go get it yourself.

My friends often offer food as a gift of love and thoughtfulness. Actress Marlene Dietrich said: "It's the friends you can call up at 4 a.m. that matter." In my case, the caring friends called at 4 a.m. to let me know they had accidentally poisoned me with dinner because they forgot about my food allergies.

The research, according to the previously mentioned Marisa G. Franco, says people who express affection for one another in the form of compliments, warm greetings and kind words become friends more quickly and those friendships endure. Don't wait to be thoughtful or caring. Don't be shy; share your feelings. Tell your friend you like her shoes!

> "A close friend is like a four-leaf clover: hard to find and lucky to have."—Irish proverb

One must always have a proverb in a document of the heart. An Irish one is all the better as there is a high likelihood that it was developed while consuming the drink in a wee pub on a rainy chilly afternoon. Can't you just envision the fellas polishing the bar with their coat sleeves and waxing on about the merits of friendship? But I digress.

You will likely have a whole range of friends in your lifetime, but it is the close friends who you need to nurture and treasure. Brooks, Gupta, Degges-White and I all agree that close friends are important to your well-being and create richness in your life. To be clear, I have based my opinion on personal experiences. The other three are referencing expert research.

I hope I have made you smile or maybe even laugh as you read this friendship story. I share joy, comfort, laughter, love and well-being with my treasured close friends.

Ruth HM

M.Ed.

I'm not an athlete but I do like to ride my bike, play golf and cross-country ski. I wear a helmet while cycling but I don't like it. I like the wind blowing through my hair. I drive a MX 5 Miata. The roof is always down except when it is raining.

I have a couple of successful independent children. I also have a couple of dogs. After some thought, I realized I am happiest when there is 100-plus pounds of dog around and my children call frequently.

I am an alumnus of both the University of Alberta and the University of Calgary. The degrees I earned at these schools coupled with some talent and creativity helped to establish a successful career in the post-secondary education system.

Writing about friendship shook loose some fun memories and enhanced my appreciation of my dear friends.

Nurturing

II. Nurturing

Relationships are that beautiful reminder of the ebb and flow of the waters of Mother Earth, with a natural progression just like the growth in our natural world (e.g plants, trees). All things need certain things to survive and grow ... just like our relationships!
—Trudy Corless

Friendship is about showing up, not just in the good times, but especially when things get tough. A true friend creates space for vulnerability, trust and growth, even when it's not easy.
—Elizabeth McQuire

The work of friendships will rejuvenate. Your heart feels full. It is a safe space, where kindness is felt and no words are required. Be. There. Trust. Forgive.
—Karen Popoff

Best friends seem to become those women who walk through it all, together. Always present is a solid foundation of trust, fierce loyalty and love.
—Shelly Bickford

Listening is a key to being a great friend. You may not even need to say anything, but to just be there and hear them with honesty, compassion and support.
—Michelle Hlady

A friend is someone who can hold space for you during your darkest moments and dance with you during the most joyful ones. Someone who celebrates you and can see your brilliance and imperfections in the same moment, and still loves you intensely, without reservation.
—Nicole van Kuppeveld

Nurturing Intergenerational Friendships

Andrea Eriksson

This is a tale of two friends of different ages — Nicole and Andrea — who formed a deep and lasting connection. It was an unlikely start to friendship, beginning with a job interview and evolving from a supervisor-and-direct-report relationship. Usually, boss-and-employee relationships are surface-level and do not expand into anything more. They span a short time during the employment period and then fizzle out with changing jobs and different life phases.

What was it about this friendship that was different? How can you, too, form a lasting friendship with someone in a different life phase? This chapter will show you how relationships can evolve beyond their initial context and how to foster deep friendships with people older or younger than you.

Why foster an intergenerational friendship?

It is important to address why having an older or young friend is valuable. People are extremely busy and only have so much time. Typically, friendships fall within the realm of what is easy or convenient. Perhaps you have children the same age, go to the same gym, or work in the same office. These friendships serve short-term needs and help people feel a sense of connection in an environment that meets their current needs. Once you leave that setting, the friendship often fades.

Intergenerational friendships offer unique perspectives and insights. Befriending someone older provides the opportunity to gain insights about navigating life phases you are approaching, such as marriage, the birth of a first child, and balancing family and career. Befriending someone younger is fulfilling as it allows you to support and give back, experiencing the excitement of life milestones anew.

Seeing yourself in another person can motivate you to help someone much younger or older as you treat them how you would like to be treated or help them as you would like to be helped. Age is just a number, and people naturally gravitate toward others like themselves. Like attracts like.

Attracting intergenerational friendships

Having an intergenerational friendship is not something that happens overnight. There must be a certain trait where you see yourself in the older or younger person. Perhaps it is the same personality profile, a common religious belief, or a similar attitude or outlook on life.

When I first started my friendship with Nicole, my former supervisor, it began with lunch to talk about our different jobs since my summer internship. There was no expectation other than to hang out and catch up. We went to lunch in the City Centre Mall, close to my new workplace. At that time, Nicole had also switched roles. We were both in different places yet found much to talk about and connect over.

The first step to deepening the friendship was made by Nicole. I was invited to help with her campaign for elected office. I was inspired that she was putting herself on the line by running for office. I walked door-to-door with her in Sherwood Park, answering questions from constituents. It was a valuable experience, not to mention we connected and talked more during those long evenings.

For an intergenerational friendship to thrive, there must be invitations into the personal sphere and introductions to older and younger peer groups. We would periodically go to Nicole's house for Friday or Saturday night campfires. It was wonderful to be invited into a new circle of family and friends and each other's personal lives. The stories, food and atmosphere were so warm on those crisp fall nights. It was during this time that our relationship shifted from former supervisor to friend. As we deepened our friendship, I invited her to my wedding and baby shower. Sharing these life milestones was special. Compatibility with the older or younger peer group is crucial for an intergenerational friendship to thrive.

I was just starting out in my marriage and had a cosy condo in a funky shopping and food district called Whyte Avenue. I might have been self-conscious about having a smaller home, but I never felt that my things were not fancy or nice enough to host a more established couple like Nicole and Gavin. A key aspect of an intergenerational friendship is connecting over shared values, interests or personalities, as the material aspects of those friendships will seldom be similar due to the age difference. This could mean bonding over a shared love of sports like bike riding or cross-country skiing, or a shared love of travelling and exploring the world.

Deepening intergenerational friendships

When an intergenerational friendship forms, it may start based on shared work, interests, and helping each other pursue common goals. However, to move to a deeper friendship, you must connect at the values level. Values are the common threads that bind people. They reflect what is really important to a person and are not dependent on what you have. They are how you operate in the world and drive your behaviour. In my intergenerational friendship with Nicole, I connected across our age difference with a similar drive for achievement, adventure, ambition, authenticity, connection, faith, family, independence, leadership and reliability. A shared value for achievement, for example, can involve helping each other reach a goal or aspiration, such as supporting a friend in authoring a book about fostering friendship.

Another aspect of deepening an intergenerational friendship is recognizing the superpowers present in relationships that allow us to connect on a deeper level. One such superpower is listening for greatness in your friend. This means recognizing their strengths, skills and aptitudes. During my wedding in 2014, I was honoured to be recognized for my event-planning abilities. After planning every last detail of my autumn wedding perfectly, I was asked to help with ideas for Nicole's 50th birthday party. We did a Sex and the City theme, had a lovely New York-themed cake and catering, and enjoyed a fun event with some of Nicole's closest friends, her mum and adult daughters. It was an honour to be involved in such a special milestone in her life. Involving your friends in meaningful ways and recognizing their talents is key to deepening an intergenerational friendship. Everyone has natural skills and aptitudes that transcend age and life experience.

Intergenerational friendships are rewarding

Next time you are looking for a friend, try finding someone outside your age group. It can be rewarding and a great way to look deeper than someone who only shares a similar life phase with you. Look for someone like you, someone who shares your values, appreciates you for who you are, and helps you shine like the gem you are.

Andrea Eriksson

Product Manager and Business Development Guru

https://www.linkedin.com/in/andrea-eriksson-469b2444/

Andrea Eriksson holds a Bachelor of Commerce from the University of Alberta and Master of Global Management from Royal Roads University. She is a business start-up and expansion specialist who enjoys creating business models and launching new projects. She is someone who easily transforms creative ideas into reality and a skilled communicator, problem-solver and project implementer. Andrea is motivated by a good challenge. Andrea has diverse work experience and has been employed in the private, non-profit, academic and government sector in organizations such as PRIMED Medical Products, NorQuest College, Edmonton Economic Development and The Business Link.

Friendship Reflections: Looking Back and Moving Forward

Nicole van Kuppeveld

I most enjoy being in the company of my friends around the campfire. When I was younger, I spent time at the family cabin on Lake Winnipeg with cousins telling stories and eating too many marshmallows. Or later in life, with my co-leaders at our Girl Guide camps with our Brownies and Guides taking in the warmth of the fire and their day. With women friends at our women's-only fire circles. Or as a couple sitting and enjoying a beautiful evening in conversation with friends from different eras and facets of our lives. Where the fire is warm and the conversations are as varied as the people joining us around our firepit. Sometimes deep, sometimes spirited, sometimes fun but never boring. The afterglow of these evenings extends until the next time we see each other or the fire draws us back together.

Some other ways are…

Being part of a women's organization

The one I belonged to gave me so much. It solidified my leadership philosophy and gave me opportunities to work on my growth edges, to create and innovate. It expanded my personal networks, possibilities and allowed me to see my potential. It showed me the power of sponsoring and amplifying women, to not only lift each other up but to do the hard work of developing our skills, to work as a united team, to create amazing community programs and profitable fundraisers. We worked tirelessly, putting on big events — like the first silent auction north of the 49th parallel — but we also learned a lot and had a lot of fun! Some of these women remain my closest friends as we continue to take on volunteer leadership roles in our community.

Volunteering

We have a friend who volunteers for an organization that provides women who have been out of work with outfits to return to the workplace. Each year, we attend a fundraiser that includes a silent auction, a fashion show and a high tea. This is a fun event that we look forward to attending annually where we get to dress up in spring dresses with fascinators — and support a great cause and justify buying auction items for charity.

I have been a volunteer in many capacities over the years. However, becoming a Girl Guide leader allowed me to share my gifts with an organization that reflected my passion for the outdoors, leadership, community service and growing the potential of young girls. The activities and camps we planned as co-leaders with and for the girls were epic. One of the co-authors talks about our Harry Potter camp in her chapter. My youngest daughter was not enamoured with having a sleepover camp at Fort Edmonton Park, where perhaps some of the stories of the past created a bit too much stimulation for her vivid imagination. Another memorable camp was an overnight camp. I invited a friend who was a potential new leader. It was the windiest night, and we had a loose flap on our tent. At one point she said: "Dorothy, are we in Kansas yet?"

Learning experiences

My lifelong commitment to learning has afforded me opportunities to meet fellow participants who were friends on a shared learning journey but whose friendships faded after our credentials were conferred. I continue to meet friends through virtual learning opportunities. I met a woman from Poland through an international online marketing course and we have initiated a friendship across the digital ocean. Another fellow participant in a recent Feminine Power course, a kindred spirit, is now an insightful business coaching partner based in the U.S. We get into a lot of deep insights, share our observations and laugh a lot (usually at ourselves) in our virtual meetings as we navigate and make course corrections in our respective businesses. Both of these relationships are instrumental in championing our respective entrepreneurial ventures.

Food & fellowship

Going out to dinner or hosting a dinner party, a BBQ or a potluck — anything that revolves around the company of friends, good food and great conversations — is usually a sure way to have fun and build connections. Food brings us together. And those sensory experiences aid in cementing the connections we build, locking them into our memories.

We started a dinner club years ago with two other couples — another fun activity that can be a way to include your partner and cultivate couple friends. So many great recipe ideas and bonding, whether it's around a friend's kitchen table, the BBQ or the fondue pot.

Going to food-tasting events, attending a cooking class together, bringing in a chef for a hands-on session or assembling bannock from baggies around a campfire are some other ways to cultivate friendships around food.

Each year, in early December, my two daughters and I host a baking bee in my kitchen. It's mostly about getting into the Christmas spirit, connecting with friends, sharing plans for the holidays, and trying out some new ideas like our Swedish Christmas menu (a departure from our traditional French Canadian dishes). It's a three-generation group, which makes for interesting conversations. The best part is that everyone gets their baking done in an afternoon and reconnects!

Fitness

Although this is not everyone's idea of fun, it is for some, including my trainer and my training partner. My weight training classes sometimes feel like a torture session, and in those, my personal trainer, friend and amateur psychologist gets the best of my 'sass.' But I am always grateful for how my body feels after the workout.

I am an avid cross-country skier, cyclist and walker (former runner) so heading out to get that adrenaline high during an aerobic workout is my idea of fun. But without my friend and training buddy who holds me accountable, I would probably find an excuse to skip my workouts. We have so many funny stories, like the guy who was skiing without a top on a sunny but crisp winter morning. And the tales on the event trails, like our half marathon running and Birkebeiner ski events, could fill a book. If you like fitness, join your local running group that gets people out to socialize while they train or allows people to find a fitness buddy. Your body and your mind will thank you for it.

Hiking. Camping. Whitewater rafting. Ski trips. All have culminated in countless memories, some breathtaking vistas and encounters with a few bears. They say that our strongest memories are of the times that we spend doing outdoor activities. So plan a picnic or a scavenger hunt with friends. Hike together. Take a trip where you ride bikes along a river, a great way to explore new cities. The smells associated with this happy event will be reignited the next time you smell a pine candle or a steak sizzling on a grill.

Shared passions

Whether you and a friend share a passion for politics or knitting (which my childhood friend is still trying to get me to do), singing, movies, books, hiking or a multitude of other things, doing something you both love or finding a new passion together is a sure way to cultivate and deepen your friendship.

Making time to do something together as friends is essential to continuing to grow closer. Our friendships need to be attended to and sharing time with a friend is a sign that you are important to one another. Your time is precious and your time together signifies that you value your friendship.

Politics is another of my passions and fledgling friendships were formed and deepened through engagement on various political committees and campaigns. During my municipal election campaign, 55 friends volunteered and dropped 5,500 brochures in our ward over three days. They were work friends, neighbours, family, friends both old and new , each invited to engage in the political process and get their walk or run in for the weekend. The camaraderie around the firepit where we warmed ourselves, drank a cold pop and gobbled a hot dog between drops was electric. The excitement about being engaged in the political process was palpable; they were proud to be showing their support for someone they deemed a worthy candidate. Someone they were committed to getting elected through their time and dedication on the campaign trail.

Work friends

I always tell people that I never ran from jobs but always ran to them. During this anthology project, I wondered if part of that pattern was having made the friends that were keepers, perhaps the draw was to a new work environment where I could cultivate more new friendships. Either way, many of the close friends in my friendship circle started out as colleagues in the workplace forged through a shared work ethic and our passion for the job. Friendships that developed through seeing their talents and having a lot of fun at work naturally moved to fun times after work hours and continued long after we moved on to other job opportunities.

One on one, two or three

Of all my friendship activities, the one I love the most is settling into a comfy chair with a cup of coffee or a glass of wine — with a close friend or two or three. These evenings are spent sharing the joys, trials and tribulations that are our lives. We roar with laughter and inevitably share tears of love, joy or sorrow. We can be our true selves — who we are in that moment. Raw, real and authentic.

If you want a friend like the friends in these stories: Be that friend. And show up for them.

As you may know, it's often hard, especially for strong women, to ask for support. So when a friend calls, know they must really need you. Make time to be there for them, arrange your schedule, make them your priority and provide them with the support they need, whether it's a listening ear, a planter of flowers, a homemade meal, a hug, a spa getaway, a friendship story for a book,—or just be there to get them through a hard moment. You'll find, as I have, that they will in turn be there for you.

At the start of this anthology, I identified the qualities that are non-negotiable for me in a friend. The qualities you seek out in a friend may be very different from mine. But know what they are. That will make it much easier to hone in on finding a lifelong friend.

My friends all bring the qualities that are important to me in a friendship: depth, authenticity, passion, adventure, learning and a love of life (joie-de-vivre) — and so many more.

My longest and closest relationships are formed by fire and conflict. If you haven't experienced and moved past some struggles together, been able to find the common ground between our divergent viewpoints, respected our differences of opinion or connected at a deep emotional level with me, our friendship won't last. I want to know the real you.

One of my sister-friends, says in her friendship chapter: "I have told others it was a relationship born of fire, but only the most brilliant and lasting gemstones form under heat and pressure." (Tracy Brandt).

The gemstones in my friendship collection are dazzling to behold. Each of you is more precious than gold — and you truly feed my soul. ♥

Walking and Talking:
The Essence of Being Vulnerable

Sue Timanson

I'm actually terrible at friendship. I have a lot of friends in my life, many acquaintances, tons of 'contacts,' but very few close friends. It's not that I don't love the friends in my life. I'm just not sure how... or maybe it's more that I don't make the time to... OK, the real truth is making, keeping, caring about a close friend is terrifying. It's a lot of work, it takes time I never feel I have, and it requires a level of honesty, vulnerability and emotional commitment that is not my strength. And that's tough for me — I'm used to being really good at whatever I do.

But enduring friendship, well, that's about being vulnerable. I can be present in every moment; I'm a good listener; I'm an excellent problem-solver. I'm empathetic. I can cheer you on, lift you up and celebrate you as my friend along with the very best of them. But be vulnerable? Pfffft. I have always thought that being vulnerable is the same as being weak, and I've never given myself the luxury of weakness.

But what my friendship with Nicole has demonstrated is that vulnerability IS strength. The strength to believe that the stronger our ties are to each other, to friendship, the stronger we become as individuals.

I don't think I'm all the way there yet, but I'm a helluva lot closer with friends like Nicole.

Work

I have a few close friends I met through work. I worked in radio for a large part of my career; not on-air, but in advertising. There were a lot of laughs, and a book's worth of adventures, but the best part of my career was a few real friendships that grew out of working together. There weren't a lot of women who worked in the radio industry when I started, so the few of us who did needed to support each other out of necessity, even when we worked for competing radio stations. We had an unspoken bond that became stronger than just work friendships, built on trust, camaraderie and support.

I still have a 'girls' weekend' every year with two of these women even though we live across the country from one another. We spend a long weekend catching up, taking some spa time and setting goals for the next year. We talk about career goals, relationship goals, personal goals… and big-stroke 'where do you see yourself' goals. It's incredibly exhausting but revitalizing at the same time. I highly recommend you find a small group of like-minded women and set some goals down in writing every year. We usually end up with eight to 15 goals each: some years are simple; some years the goals are heavy, but every year it absolutely stuns me to see how many we achieve.

Every year, I only look at them the week before the next goal-planning weekend, terrified to see how few I can cross off the list, only to be shocked at how many I've achieved. It's the power of writing it down! And the power of trusting friends, to be honest with you, challenge you, and believe in you. See, I do know how… if pushed to it.

Soccer

I've played soccer since I was eight years old and it's always been my 'quiet place.' It's the one place I can go, whether I'm playing or coaching, where I don't have to think about anything else, just what's on the field. I don't have to worry about what others think or see or expect of me; I can just be focused on winning a soccer game.

More than one person has looked at my schedule or the responsibilities or the expectations, and told me, "Well, it's obvious that you're going to have to give up soccer." And my response to them is that my time at or on the soccer field is the one place where the only expectations I feel are my own. Everyone needs to have a place or space where they can say that.

Politics

Hmmm... where to start? I'll start with the very best thing that has come out of my political activism: my friendship with Nicole. It's brought me other good friends and a community of like-minded people, but none of them come close to my relationship with Nicole.

We first met when I was running for a provincial candidate nomination and she was the constituency president who presided over the election process. We formed a bond then and although I didn't win the nomination, we became friends. The next touch-point was when she was a federal nomination candidate and I worked on her campaign. Our friendship and trust in each other grew. A couple of years later, I was successful in becoming a candidate in a provincial election and she stepped up to be my campaign manager. She was magnificent in that role — demanding and encouraging, and as devastated as I was when we didn't win. But our bond was solidified and I can never thank her enough.

Our friendship has survived and grown far beyond politics. I've supported her and she's supported me, although I think I've tested her commitment far beyond patience. LOL! And our friendship has grown to include our husbands, who are probably the best two 'sign guys' (IYKYK) in all of Alberta, and whose commitment to the campaigns I will always appreciate.

We love our invitations to the infamous fire pit evenings with a growing circle of friends, and couple-dates and catch-ups.

Next

Although our friendship grew out of a political connection, it has thrived on a commitment to be there for each other and I have learned to trust in the time we spend together. We briefly worked together last year, which I thought went pretty well, especially for two pretty strong-minded-used-to-being-in-charge women. I believe our friendship actually grew from the experience. I know our trust in each other grew and I realized then just how much I can rely on her being there for me.

One of the things I love most is our walks, and I know there are days when Nicole and I 'walk and talk' where it's probably Nicole's third walk of the day. But she never complains and still walks faster than me! On many days, these walks have been timely for us both, and I value the advice or sometimes the admonishment or just plain encouragement we offer each other.

I know Nicole has many others who rely on her to listen, to hear and to support them. I hope I offer her a place where she can also be heard, supported and uplifted. After all, that's what friends are for. At least, that's what they tell me.

I still think I'm not great at friendship, but I am incredibly lucky that my friends, especially Nicole, are very, very good at it. And I'm grateful for her every day.

Sue Timanson

Strathcona Community Hospital Foundation
Executive Director

https://www.linkedin.com/in/sue-timanson-03814925/
https://www.facebook.com/sue.timanson
https://www.instagram.com/suetimanson/

I am the Executive Director of the Strathcona Community Hospital Foundation, a role that perfectly blends my passion for community and deep commitment to helping others.

With almost 40 years of experience in leadership, politics and communications, I have a knack for building lasting relationships and creating strong, effective teams. But beyond my professional life, I'm wife to Kent, my lifelong love, a proud Mum and a doting Nana.

Sports have long been an integral part of my life. A lifelong fan, I also play soccer and have since I was eight. And coaching women's soccer is one of my greatest joys. The field is my quiet place, and I value every moment. Sport embodies the teamwork, mutual support and respect I cherish in every facet of my life. I've formed lifelong bonds of friendship through work, politics and sport. And I hold these friends close.

Dementia's Journey:
A United Front for Person-Centred Care

Renate Sainsbury

Our friendship started at work in the psychiatry department at the Misericordia Hospital in Edmonton, Alberta. I was the first recreation therapist to work in acute care, and working with strong health professionals in this role was very intimidating.

Nicole was the occupational therapist and very confident in her role working in psychiatry. She helped me feel more confident in what I had to offer. We ran a cooking program together. One day, I was making pizza with some clients and a small fire in the oven set off the fire alarm. We had to evacuate the kitchen area and the firefighters came into the unit. We heard about that from the unit manager!

The kitchen fire was the real event that set us up as friends as we were in it together. We really enjoyed the clients we worked with in our recreation and OT programs. Thinking back, Nicole helped me build my confidence working in psychiatry, supported me and taught me so much.

I also recall going to visit her when she lived by the university. We had some deep conversations about life and things that we could look forward to in the future (like our grandsons). Eventually, we left for other jobs, to build our respective businesses and raise our families.

Although we did not see each other, periodically we connected through others, as we had mutual professional contacts who kept us informed of each other's newest ventures.

Fast forward three decades.

We reconnected when I learned that her brother had passed. She was able to talk with me about the loss and the lack of assistance from health-care providers to prevent his death by suicide.

We were both from Sherwood Park, loved our family and suffered losses in our lives, including my daughter Jackie, who died too young from a medical error. Despite these and other losses, we were able to become more flexible, thoughtful, resourceful and forward-thinking.

Neither of us is afraid to open ourselves up and speak the truth and fight for a more just health-care system focused on person-centred care, well-being, prevention education and community focus. Organizational cultural change in health care cannot happen if one keeps quiet and does not speak the truth. We have been women warriors for human-centred health care throughout our professional careers. I decided that if the assisted living and memory care facilities were not person-centred, I would build my own. In partnership with a local developer, we co-founded Lifestyle Option person-centred care centres that are used for placements by our local health authority.

A few years ago, Nicole needed assistance with her father, who was diagnosed with dementia. She reached out to me because of my understanding of caring for the elderly and my assisted living experience. She needed a road map and a guide. I was that person. I listened and provided resources and support.

Our collaboration resulted in finding the right place for her father to live, where love, care and compassion are at the root of life in the care home. Her father ended up in one of the care homes that I own and was instrumental in developing. It included a dementia care model we brought to Canada from the U.K.

In the course of Nicole's dementia journey with her father, I introduced her to Bernie and Jody, two of my friends. We all wanted a more citizen-centred approach with individuals living with dementia being part of the community (not being warehoused in institutions). We are the risk-takers and want human justice for all.

Bernie, who recently died of cancer, was the founder of the Early Onset Dementia Alberta Foundation. She was passionate about the lived experience of people with dementia, as her husband was diagnosed with dementia in his 50s and she struggled to keep him at home as long as possible. There came a point when he had to be put into a nursing home and unfortunately, he was overmedicated. Bernie's advocacy and determination resulted in him being moved into an acute rehabilitation facility, where he was taken off medication and was able to get around in his wheelchair, drink and eat by himself. He would have died in the original care centre had she not taken him out. He was later placed into a facility that fosters person-centred care for persons living with dementia. Bernie and I sat on a committee created by Alberta Health to develop a provincial (state) dementia strategy.

Jody was Bernie's devoted friend who walked alongside her in their shared journey, with spouses diagnosed with early onset dementia. She too was an advocate for people with dementia. She was in charge of education sessions offered through the Early Onset Dementia Alberta Foundation and both Bernie and Jody ran education and conferences to challenge old ways of institutional care for people with dementia. When Jody's husband had to go into care, he was placed in Lifestyle Options Whitemud, one of my assisted living facilities that uses the butterfly model of care, which was started by Dr. David Sheard from the U.K. It works on the premise that feelings matter for each individual member of the care community.

In this model, the staff get to eat with the residents to know each individual and their families and find out their history and what matters. This experience is very important, to allow the residents to live well with dementia, with meaning and purpose. The environment is full of colour and the stuff of life that matters to them is in their own rooms as a reminder to staff about what is important. Each unit has access to the outdoors, allowing care clients to get outside in rain, sunshine or snow.

Strength, self-esteem, and courage are what bonded me with friends like Nicole, Bernie and Jody. We take risks and are not afraid to speak out and advocate for others. Yet we are always able to see the humour in life, like the kitchen fire fiasco. We can also open ourselves up to being vulnerable with each other during significant losses, which has cemented our friendships.

I am forever grateful to have friends who understand, listen and take action for others to build a better future.

Renate Sainsbury

Retired Co-Founder Lifestyle Options Retirement Communities
Advocate

https://www.linkedin.com/in/renate-sainsbury-3a77b245/
https://www.facebook.com/renate.sainsbury
https://www.instagram.com/renatesainsbury/
https://meaningfulcarematters.com/
https://lifestyleoptions.ca/

I am an advocate for better care and services for individuals living with dementia and also better health care for all, with a focus on person-centred care. Each individual has abilities and meaning if we can harness these, by focusing on the social determinants of health we will be able to shift a system from ill-being to well-being.

It is about connections based on love, attachment and real engagement where every life matters, where people come first, not systems. Never doubt that a small group of thoughtful committed citizens can change the world; indeed, it's the only thing that ever has. -Margaret Mead

The Mystery and Profound Impact of Friendships

Melanie Nakatsui

Life has a way of surprising us, particularly when we least expect it. Sometimes these surprises are the result of choices we make; sometimes they are the result of circumstances beyond our control. Some of the best surprises in my life have been the development of deep friendships. When it happens, we don't always know how or why — but we know the feeling is incredible. As someone whose love language is giving — time, resources or simply a listening ear — I have come to realize how impactful friendships are in life. For me, they are one of life's wonderful surprises that present as gifts — gifts of connection, joy, and shared experiences that shape who we become.

As I grow older, I have learned that the presence we offer one another is much more important than the words we exchange. This realization is captured in a line from the movie Dune: Part One that has served as an inspiration to me: "The mystery of life isn't a problem to solve, but a reality to experience."

Many people might read this as simply expressing how unpredictable life can be, but for me, it resonates with the essence of friendship. It serves as a powerful reminder that our connections with others are not about finding the perfect solution or saying the right words. Instead, they are about being present, embracing the journey, and finding joy in the shared experiences that make life so rich and fulfilling.

Like life itself, friendship cannot be understood or analyzed. It is a living, breathing thing that evolves with time in response to the experiences we go through and the moments we treasure. It's about appreciating the relationships we forge and accepting the journey with all its ups and downs.

Throughout my life, I have been drawn to others who share my values — kindness, empathy and compassion. This includes being in the company of people who genuinely care about you and let you be yourself without fear of criticism — a place where vulnerability is revealed and the cone of silence is guarded. Those who are kind, caring and empathetic, and who recognize the value of giving without expecting anything in return, are the people I consider to be truly close. Being asked to contribute to this friendship anthology by my dear friend Nicole makes me feel incredibly honoured and happy.

Nicole exemplifies all the traits I value most, including a willingness to serve others. Even though we don't see each other as much as we'd like, every time we get together it seems like no time has passed. By being herself, Nicole has a way of making you feel heard, noticed and appreciated. Whether we are working together on a project or simply enjoying a cup of coffee, my friend's presence is always calming and reassuring. We don't need to say much; actions and demeanour speak volumes. She has my sincerest gratitude for organizing this anthology where we can celebrate friendship.

I have found that friendship is not something we can force or manufacture. It has to happen naturally. With close friends, our conversations flow effortlessly, but the true beauty of friendship is in the moments of silence — the feeling of being heard and understood, the unspoken bond that is shared in quietness, allowing the relationship to evolve naturally, without the need for constant analysis or intervention. These are the moments that make friendship so special.

One of the most memorable experiences I've had with my friends was during a particularly difficult time in my life. I had recently lost a loved one and I was struggling to cope with the grief and sadness that enveloped me. Their offers of support had a profound impact on my quality of life. Simply listening and letting me express my feelings without judgment were truly appreciated. Empathy and understanding were exactly what I needed, and I will always be grateful for the unwavering support of my close circle of friends during this challenging time. I also learned during that time how to be a better friend to others in my life. Only in our darkest moments do we truly know that we are always here for each other.

Each special person in my life is unique and together, we form a bond that is unlike any other. It is a great and beautiful web that ties us together. When we are able to introduce one of our friends to another, and they form a special bond, it is a very rewarding feeling, knowing that other friendships can develop through your connection.

One of the greatest lessons I've learned in life and with my friendships is the importance of giving without expecting anything in return. In a world that often prioritizes self-interest and competition, there is something truly special about those who give freely of their time, energy and resources where they can. These are the people who make life's journey more enjoyable, and they help us navigate the inevitable challenges and uncertainties that come our way.

I have many beautiful friends who exemplify this kind of selflessness. They are always willing to lend a helping hand, whether it's through volunteering with me, helping me, listening or simply being there when needed. I happily do the same for my family and friends, and it is an honour to be able to do so. Generosity of spirit has not only strengthened my friendships but has also inspired me to consider other ways in which I can support people. As I continue on my own journey, I have come to embrace the idea that life's enigmas are opportunities to grow and learn. Instead of seeking out people who fit a specific mould or meet certain criteria, I believe in the beauty of each unique connection, recognizing that every friendship brings something valuable to my life and hopefully the other way around as well.

For example, some of my closest friends are those who challenge me to see the world from a different perspective. We may not always agree and our conversations can sometimes be spirited, but it is through these interactions that I have gained a deeper understanding of myself and the world around me. These friendships have taught me the importance of being open to new ideas and experiences, and sometimes push me out of my comfort zone.

Other friendships are more grounded in shared experiences and common interests. These connections are built on the things we enjoy doing together. But even with these friendships, I have learned that the true value lies not in the activities themselves, but in the moments of connection and understanding that happen along the way.

One of the most rewarding aspects of friendship is the way it evolves over time. As we grow and change, so do our friendships. Some connections may deepen and become more meaningful, while others may fade or take on a different form. But through it all, the mystery of friendship remains — a reminder that life is not something to be solved or controlled, but something to be experienced and enjoyed.

Trust and loyalty are fundamental to any meaningful friendship. Bonds are built when we can rely on one another, knowing that our words are held in confidence. Being vulnerable with someone is not easy; it requires courage and a deep sense of security. When we trust that our thoughts and feelings won't be misconstrued or shared with others, we open ourselves to deeper connections. This mutual understanding and respect solidify a true friendship.

Another fascinating aspect is that the emotional connection in friendship goes beyond shared experiences and mutual trust; it also involves brainwave synchronization. Studies have shown that when close friends interact and are 'on the same wavelength,' their brainwaves can align. Such alignment presumably reflects emotional resonance between friends, creating a sense of being truly understood and connected. When friends share a laugh or a moment of silence, their brains are not just reacting to the stimulus but are attuning to each other, reinforcing the emotional ties that define their relationship.

This neural connection is a testament to the depth of human relationships, demonstrating how friendships can shape our mental and emotional states, leading to a profound sense of belonging and mutual support. I am grateful for the emotional connections I have made along the way.

As I look back on the friendships that have shaped my life, I am filled with gratitude for the people who have walked alongside me in my journey. Kindness, compassion and support have been a constant in all of my friendships. All my friends have truly inspired me; each connection has added depth and meaning to my life in ways that words alone cannot capture.

Cherish the moments of connection, the shared silences and the unspoken understanding that make friendship one of life's greatest gifts. I embrace the mystery, knowing that it is in the experience of life itself that we find the deepest meaning and fulfilment.

Melanie Nakatsui

Founder of Nakatsui SKIN

https://www.facebook.com/NakatsuiDerm
https://www.instagram.com/melanie_nakatsui
https://www.instagram.com/nakatsuiderm
https://www.instagram.com/nakatsuiskin
https://nakatsuiderm.com
https://nakatsuiskin.com

Melanie Nakatsui is first and foremost a loving mother, wife, daughter, sister, cousin, friend and confidante. Her life revolves around her family and friends, and she takes pride in nurturing and supporting those she loves. Melanie creates a welcoming environment wherever she goes. She spends her professional time nurturing Nakatsui DermaSurgery, Nakatsui SKIN, and the Thomas and Melanie Nakatsui Family Fund.

Her dedication to her family, friends and her staff is matched by her commitment to the community. She is actively involved in various charitable initiatives, striving to make a positive impact, particularly with the Lois Hole Hospital Women's Society and the Edmonton Opera. She thoroughly enjoys spending time with her husband, Thomas, and her daughter, Natalie. Whether she is lending a listening ear, offering advice, or simply being there in times of need, Melanie's presence is a source of comfort to those who know her best.

Finding a Pet Sitter and a Sister Friend

Rose Dunlop

I met Nicole through a mutual hairdresser. Nicole was looking for a pet sitter for her precious dog Ronan and the hairdresser referred her to me for my pet-sitting services.

When I met her, I was attracted to her honesty and her compassion for Ronan and as I later learned, her compassion for everyone in her life. I admired her devotion to self-care and exercise. It was fun getting to know her and to meet Ronan!

Our friendship has flourished quickly, with dinners, backyard fires, intimate talks, coffee on the deck and walks with and without Ronan.

Similar ideologies

We shared similarities that we found in our adult children. This realization was profound for me, and the support and conversations we had were healing. I did not feel alone in my views, experiences and opinions about my adult son anymore.

Together we are walking alongside each other through this new phase in our lives as grandmothers seeking to negotiate new relationships with our children, two of whom are now parents. We share similarities and triumphs as we carefully negotiate toward our goal of a stronger parent-to-parent connection and the possibility of a meaningful friendship (like the ones described in this book) with them.

I am learning that Nicole and I share similar ideologies when it comes to work ethic. I admire Nicole's academic achievements and the constant dedication she applies to everything she does, like her women's coaching and leadership development company. I worked as a travel nurse and she was an occupational therapist, so our health-care background is another area we share and apply to all of the friends and seniors in our lives.

At home

I am so fortunate to pet-sit Ronan and care for Nicole and Gavin's home and yard while they are travelling. I'm not going to lie: some things irritate the crap out of me – like their very expensive, five-star coffee pot. Well, this machine and I do not do well together. You have to grind the beans, set up the filter and the pot just right, and more than once, I have flooded the entire counter with grinds and brewed coffee that never made it into my cup. That's when my $15 French press comes to the rescue. Or I do a coffee run to Tim Hortons.

Then, there is their central vacuum system. After 10 attempts, I think I have it figured out, saving me from having to run home and get my trusted Bissell. That's the beauty of their location. It's only a short drive to my place, where I dwell in a condo that welcomes the parking lot from the porch, and the dust, Uber drop-offs and Skip the Dishes. And where every single solitary soul thinks I'm the welcoming committee and my patio is the hospitality suite for the complex.

I get respite at Nicole's, so peaceful and private, a home where I have 10 more windows than my two, a beautiful backyard that is like a park, the hot tub and my honey Ronan!

Ronan

Let's talk about Ronan. I think he is part pit bull, part lab, mountain something and a wee bit of wolf. He is absolutely stunning, which is the reason people stop us on every walk or in every off-leash area to comment on his beautiful face. And that is why Nicole refers to him as Ronan the Handsome.

Ronan had a rather difficult start, abandoned by his mommy at two weeks old with his littermates, in two foster homes before he came into Nicole and Gavin's home at five weeks, then surgery for a valve repair at six months. Ronan has had experiences with a couple of different trainers.

The first time I met him, I thought I was going to faint, his bark was so intimidating. I was thinking, "Holy crap, what have I gotten myself into?" But I thought, "maybe he needs me as much as I need him." So we got to work — meet-and-greets, walks and a private 'dancing' session for me with the intense (good-looking) trainer. I liked that very much, lol.

As Ronan and I bonded, and we spent more time together, it was becoming clear that Ronan is a very smart dog but he has some fears. I decided I was going to walk beside him, be his person in his mommy's absence, be there for him and help him explore his unknown. I'm so grateful I did.

Dog whisperer

I grew up on a small farm in Ontario. We had many different animals: ponies, horses, pigs, chickens, ducks, cats and dogs.

I remember my father and brothers working with the horses but not so much with the dogs. Our dogs were always well-behaved and we didn't have a trainer. I learned rather quickly that positive attention equals positive behaviour.

I can remember coming over to Nicole's for coffee, and trying to remember, do I knock on the door? Do I ring the doorbell? Do I open the door or wait? What to do to support his training regime? Whatever it was or wasn't, I thought if I felt the pressure, how did Ronan feel? Well, with a combined approach of clear expectations for behaviour, clear commands – like 'mat' for going to the mat when the doorbell rings – positive reinforcement and gentle guidance, he figured it out.

On one pet-sitting experience at Ronan's, I threw a load of clothes in the washer and left the big jug of Tide too close to the edge of the washing machine and it fell off, leaking that nice thick soap all over the basement floor. Ronan knew it had happened – he was trying to get my attention and he wanted me to go downstairs. It took him a few tries to get my attention but he did, of course, and he was rewarded with positive feedback. I thought to myself, if it takes him a bit of time to communicate something to me, I can give him the same respect in return.

I was actually pet-sitting Ronan while writing this chapter. We had a rather fierce windstorm and it took the umbrella out of the patio table and the table shattered into pieces all over the deck. I was worried about Ronan stepping on glass, as I was cleaning shards out of my hands and knees, but once again, our bright boy knew and he patiently waited for me to clear a pathway for him to access the backyard for his business. I was truly devastated. But when Nicole returned, she was very understanding and grateful for the time it took me to clean up the glass. She made light of it and said they needed a new table anyway.

Another time, I loaded up Ronan in the crate in the back of my Rav and off we went to one of our favourite places for a scratch-and-sniff hike. Down the road two minutes, and Ronan was whining and shaking. I looked down at my dashboard and noticed the back hatch wasn't completely closed, so again, Ronan shone through with his brightness. We still have some work to do with social skills, but with kindness and patience, we will get there. Over the time I've known Ronan (about 1.5 years), he has matured a great deal. He is a very good boy. A sweet and sensitive boy. A smart boy. And a very handsome boy!

If you haven't guessed, I am instinctively comfortable with animals and small children, but adults are a very different story. Why is this? Well, trauma after trauma doesn't heal a traumatized person. But special dogs and special people do.

Sharing is caring

Nicole shares her vulnerability and authenticity with me and others openly and honestly. She effortlessly provides a safe place for others to do the same without judgment.

I shared some of my experiences with Nicole, which I must confess was not an easy thing for me to do. Nicole allowed the space and the compassion, and for the first time in a long time, I really felt safe. Someone was really listening. I am so grateful to have found a sister-friend in Nicole.

Nicole is the most giving person, ready and willing to help anyone who crosses her path. We embarked on coursework by Claire Zammit focused on empowering women and breaking down inner barriers. I feel so fortunate to share this with Nicole and to learn alongside her on this journey of feminine power. I feel that completion of this course is going to be life-changing for me. And it will allow me to move forward in life adventures with a new mindset. And it's going to be great for her clients.

If you knew Nicole's mother Louise, you would understand where Nicole's strength and compassion were cultivated. One of the things I most admire about Nicole is the close, loving relationship she shares with her mother. It is beautiful to witness this kind of mother-and-daughter relationship that has blossomed into a special friendship over the years. I am grateful to have them and to be a part of their family.

A part of the family

I quickly became friends with Louise and Andy, Nicole's father, both when Nicole was home and when she was away on vacation. The friendship was immediate. It felt like we had known each other our entire lives, not only with Louise and Andy, but with Nicole too.

Louise is a brilliant and vibrant young woman in her 80s. I can't express in words how much I respect this woman; she teaches me something every time I talk to her. Let's be honest – we really do laugh, and we cry too. Sometimes, the curveball life throws is challenging.

I had the honour of visiting Andy in his residence, where he lives due to his dementia diagnosis. He didn't know me, but he enjoyed our visit because he felt my caring vibration. I have had some experience with long-term care, dementia and Alzheimer's. I know it's difficult for Nicole's family, but what people don't understand is that it is not that hard or horrible for the person with the diagnosis. You have to train yourself to be in their world at that moment.

The moral of this friendship story is that perhaps we should meet people where they are at each moment, instead of trying to motivate them to go where we want them to go or who we want them to be. Nicole demonstrates this practice and full presence, holding space for those who are open to allowing themselves to be vulnerable, with great ease. Nicole is a wise old soul. She has been a great role model to me and many others.

"To be beautiful means to be yourself. You don't need to be accepted by others. You need to accept yourself." -Thich Nhat Hanh

Rose Dunlop

I was born and raised in a small town in Ontario, the youngest of nine children.

I was a registered nurse (RN) for 34 years. A lot of those years I was a travelling RN in the U.S. I met a lot of people and lived in some awesome places.

I enjoy nature, kayaking, the beach, swimming and yoga.

I have one son, a beautiful daughter-in-law and two precious grandsons here in Edmonton, which is the reason I moved here in 2021.

Kindred Spirits of the Digital Ocean

Betty Gotwald

The Digital Ocean, a vast and dynamic expanse of opportunities, can be both exhilarating and overwhelming. It's a realm where innovation thrives, where dreams intertwine with technology, and where connections are forged in the ethereal space between ones and zeros. Yet, amidst the ebb and flow of this digital tide, genuine friendships can emerge, sometimes in the most unexpected of circumstances. This was the case with Betty Gotwald, an Artificial Intelligence (AI) marketing coach with a passion for empowering others through technology, and Nicole van Kuppeveld, a leadership coach and kindred spirit whose warmth and unwavering support would prove to be a guiding light in Betty's journey.

Their paths first intertwined within the confines of an international online learning platform, a virtual space designed for growth and transformation. However, instead of finding the promised guidance and empowerment, in this program they encountered a disappointing reality of unmet expectations and a sense of being misled. This shared experience, a crucible of frustration and disappointment, unexpectedly laid the groundwork for an extraordinary friendship.

In the aftermath of this shared disillusionment, a spark of connection ignited between Betty and Nicole. A common enemy, a shared sense of injustice, had brought them together. Betty's expertise in AI and marketing and a heart full of compassion recognized Nicole's potential and extended professional AI marketing support. Nicole, a natural leader with a gentle spirit, offered her insights on leadership and personal development, helping Betty navigate the complexities of both the digital world and the human heart.

Their connection deepened beyond the realm of professional collaboration. They became confidantes, sharing the triumphs and tribulations of their entrepreneurial journeys through the Digital Ocean. Betty, who has dedicated her life to helping others harness the power of AI for marketing and personal manifestation, found solace in Nicole's constant support and gentle guidance. Nicole, in turn, discovered a kindred spirit in Betty as someone who understood the challenges and joys of navigating the digital landscape.

Betty's work as an AI marketing coach was a testament to her passion for empowering others. She helps individuals and businesses unlock the potential of AI to create stunning visuals and compelling narratives, guiding them toward manifesting their dreams through the power of technology. Nicole, a women-centred leadership coach with a keen understanding of human nature, had an absolute belief in Betty's abilities, and she became an invaluable source of encouragement.

Their friendship blossomed into a safe haven, a space where they could shed the masks they wore in the digital world and reveal their true selves. Nicole, with her quiet strength and kindness, played a pivotal role in Betty's personal growth. She gently nudged Betty to confront her fears and vulnerabilities, never allowing her to retreat into isolation. Nicole's belief in Betty's potential inspired her to become a better friend, a more empathetic listener and a more compassionate human being.

Their journey together was a tapestry woven with countless threads of connection, shared laughter and silent understanding. They celebrated each other's victories, large and small, offering comfort in moments of loss and weathering the storms of life side by side. Through it all, their friendship deepened, becoming a beacon of light in the often-turbulent waters of the Digital Ocean.

Betty, eternally grateful for Nicole's presence in her life, often reflected on the profound impact their friendship had on her. Nicole's gentle guidance and her belief in Betty's abilities had transformed her in countless ways. She was a more confident leader, a more empowered individual and a more compassionate friend because of Nicole's influence.

Their story is a testament to the power of human connection in the digital age, a reminder that even in the vastness of the online world, genuine friendships can flourish. It is a tale of shared dreams and mutual respect, an example of the enduring power of the human spirit to connect and uplift even in the most unexpected of circumstances.

As Betty and Nicole continue their journey through the Digital Ocean, their friendship remains a constant source of strength and inspiration. It is a reminder that true connection can transcend the boundaries of the digital world and that kindred spirits can find each other and forge bonds that will last a lifetime. And so, to Nicole, Betty extends her heartfelt gratitude. Thank you for being the friend she needed, the guiding light that illuminated her path, and the champion who helped her navigate the complexities of life and the ever-evolving landscape of the digital world. Your friendship is a treasure, a gift that Betty will forever cherish.

Betty Gotwald

CEO of VANAHAIM Marketing

https://www.linkedin.com/in/bettygotwald/
https://www.facebook.com/DrBettyQuantumAI
https://www.bettygotwald.com
https://www.vanahaim.com/youraipics

Dr. Betty Gotwald, known as CaptAIn Betty, is a pioneering expert in Quantum AI, specializing in empowering spiritual entrepreneurs to harness the power of AI in their businesses. With over a decade of business and academic experience, Dr. Betty transformed her own career by integrating AI-powered marketing tools, mindset strategies and cutting-edge technology. She's renowned for helping bold businesswomen attract more online clients without the stress of traditional social media marketing.

As a talented AI-supercharged photo creator, Dr. Betty revolutionizes content creation and reclaims precious time for family and personal life. She's passionate about showing women how to achieve their big dreams without sacrificing their health or family. Having served over 5,000 clients and witnessed profound transformations, Dr. Betty is dedicated to guiding others in making waves in the world, blending the potential of AI with the human spirit for a fulfilling, impactful business journey.

A Rare Gem

Zyrha Nielsen Clemente

Our story began in a time of uncertainty. I found myself staring at my phone in desperate need of a client for my virtual assistant services when the opportunity to work in this capacity for Nicole presented itself. She was my boss but little did I know she would soon become much more than that.

Our journey started with some challenges. I was hired as a virtual assistant but my knowledge of managing a virtual office was limited. At the same time, I was navigating through personal family issues: a delicate balance that seemed impossible to maintain. In the first week of my employment, my laptop broke, leaving me to rely on an outdated phone. Communicating and delivering work through this antiquated device across a 15-hour time zone difference between Canada and the Philippines was a struggle. The embarrassment of my situation made it difficult for me to confess to her that I lacked the proper tools to do my job effectively.

A virtual assistant without a device? The irony did not escape me.

Nicole saw how much I was struggling. Instead of getting frustrated, she showed kindness: she offered me a new device. This was more than a technical fix; it felt like a lifeline. Her caring and supportive nature was clear in that moment and it made me even more determined not to disappoint her. I realized how lucky I was to have met someone virtually who brought positivity to every interaction in the work we did together under the contract for my services.

Nicole has become more than my boss; she is a mentor, a friend and sometimes a therapist. We share personal stories and her advice is always perfect. Her wisdom helps me deal with many challenges. Her constant support and good advice got me through tough times. If I had to describe her I'd use words like appreciative, brilliant, co-operative, kind, creative, determined, friendly, hardworking, supportive and thoughtful. Any positive word would fit. Her words and actions calm me and help me find peace during hard times.

She is like an older sister to me. I admire her, look to her for advice and value her words. She supports my choices personally and professionally and always guides me in the right direction. The love, openness, connection and wisdom she shares make her one of the best people in my life.

Over time, we have shared more of our personal lives with each other. Even though we have never met in person, our online talks are meaningful and memorable. The trust we have built keeps us close. We create a space where we can be honest without fear of judgment. This trust and respect make our relationship special. We celebrate each other's successes, help each other through setbacks and always check in on each other.

One of the best parts of our relationship is our shared love for learning. We love exchanging new ideas and resources, learning and brainstorming together. This is one of the foundations of our connection. Nicole is one of my learning buddies. We attend webinars and take online courses to improve our skills. Our learning journeys are intertwined, each step taken in unison, propelling us and the business forward. She encourages me to push past my limits and believe in myself.

Reflecting on our journey, I realize how much we have learned from each other. Her wisdom and guidance have been invaluable, shaping me into a better person and professional. I am grateful for every moment we have shared and look forward to many more to come. Our friendship is a rare gem, one that I cherish deeply. In the future, whether we finally meet in person or continue our online friendship, one thing is certain: our friendship will last. It has survived time and distance, proving that true connections go beyond physical boundaries.

As our professional relationship grew, we found a shared love for creative projects. She encouraged me to take on tasks outside my comfort zone, helping me grow. Whether it was designing a new marketing strategy or tackling a complex project, she always believed in my abilities. She celebrated every success, no matter how small, and helped me see setbacks as chances to learn and improve.

Her influence goes beyond professional advice. She has played a crucial role in my personal development, offering insights that helped me navigate difficult situations in my personal life. During one particularly challenging time, her support was unwavering. She listened without judgment, offered practical advice and gave me a new perspective on the situation. Her balance of empathy and practicality is one of the many reasons I value her guidance.

As we worked together, we began to dream about a future where our collaboration would reach new heights. We talked about potential projects, new skills to learn and ways to innovate in our field. These conversations weren't just about work; they were about our shared dreams and goals. Her enthusiasm inspires me to think bigger and aim higher. Together, we set ambitious yet achievable goals, knowing we have each other's support every step of the way.

Our journey has had its challenges. There were times when projects didn't go as planned, deadlines were missed or external circumstances created obstacles. In these moments, her calm and composed demeanour reassured me. She approaches problems with a solution-oriented mindset, always focusing on what we could learn rather than what went wrong. Her ability to stay positive and proactive isa lesson in resilience and leadership.

Nicole's encouragement is a constant source of motivation. She sees my potential even when I doubt myself. Her faith in my abilities pushes me to strive for excellence and take on challenges I would have otherwise avoided. She has a unique way of giving constructive feedback, ensuring I learn and grow from every experience. Her words are always kind yet honest, helping me see my strengths and areas for improvement.

Our relationship is built on mutual respect and admiration. Nicole values my contributions and always makes me feel like an important part of the team. Her leadership style is inclusive and empowering, fostering an environment where creativity and collaboration thrive. Working with Nicole has led me to become more confident in my abilities, more resilient in the face of challenges, and more open to new experiences. Looking back, I can see how much I have grown and I owe much of this to her influence.

Amidst the hard work and challenges, there are countless moments of laughter and joy. We share jokes, funny stories and light-hearted banter that make even the toughest days brighter. These moments are essential to balancing work demands and maintaining a positive outlook. Nicole's sense of humour has brought warmth and camaraderie to our interactions.

The most remarkable aspect of our relationship is how it has thrived despite the physical distance. We have built a deep and meaningful connection through online interactions alone. This speaks to the strength of our bond and the genuine nature of our relationship. Our story is a testament to the power of human relationships in the digital age.

The future is bright with possibilities. We look forward to new adventures, new projects and new milestones. The path ahead is unknown, but with her as a treasured friend, I am confident that we will navigate it with the same resilience, trust and support that have defined our friendship journey so far.

I am deeply grateful for Nicole's presence in my life. She has been a light in dark times, a source of strength when I felt weak and a well of wisdom when I needed guidance. Our friendship is a gift that I treasure every day. I look forward to many more years of learning, growing and thriving together.

Our story is far from over; it has only just begun.

Zyrha Nielsen Clemente

Organizations by Design Inc.
Office Manager

https://www.linkedin.com/in/zyrha-clemente-9a492a232/
https://www.facebook.com/zyrhanielsen.clemente
https://www.instagram.com/zyrhaclemente

I am an aspiring marketing professional with a passion for learning and growth. Guided by the motto "It is what it is," I embrace both the good and bad in life, believing that everything happens for a reason and offers valuable lessons. This philosophy helps me navigate challenges and opportunities with a positive outlook, always eager to learn and evolve.

Through my journey in marketing and personal growth, I strive to create and maintain relationships that are built on trust, support and authenticity. These connections are the cornerstone of my life, and I am grateful for the lessons and love they bring.

Sustaining

III. Sustaining

A life-long friend is a soul sister, someone you share a connection with that cannot erode even through the ups and downs of a lifetime.
—**Kim Krushell**

Your people, you will know them and be drawn to them. They have qualities you admire; they inspire you. Nurture the relationship with time, laughter and allow the shedding of tears. Respectfully navigate challenges. This will create a meaningful bond, no matter the distance and time.
—**Karen Popoff**

What I am learning lately from my adult friends is resilience. I see these women deal with illness, deaths, demanding jobs, demanding people and demanding lives. Yet somehow we are able to continue to feel the love and support we share. And laughs – we still seem to be able to laugh at life!
—**Maureen Landry**

Cherish the memories of past friendships, the memories you will continue to make with present friends and the new memories with future friends you haven't yet met.
—**Shannon Brice**

Workout Buddies to Soulmates: Unexpected Shared Experiences

Ian McKay

Acquaintance, friend, good friend, best friend. For children that progression probably happens in a few days. For me, and probably most adults, it is a much slower process. You might not even realize when you begin to think of someone as a friend rather than an acquaintance or a good friend versus a casual friend. Occasionally, if you are fortunate, you do remember some of those points on the journey.

I consider myself lucky that I remember exactly when I began to think of Nicole as a very special friend.

I was sitting outside the intensive care unit at a local hospital where my wife Jaye was gravely ill. I made all the necessary phone calls to let family and friends know the situation. Our son was with me, but he had to be moving constantly so would disappear for long periods. As I sat there alone, I began to feel the need for a shoulder to cry on, a hug, someone to talk to and a calming presence. It was Nicole who I reached out to, in large part because after several years of working out together three days a week, I just found her so easy to talk to.

When I contacted her, her immediate response was "I will be there as soon as possible." And she was. I have no idea what she needed to reorganize but she did it. She even showed up armed with a clean shirt, a toothbrush, a comb and probably other things as well. But it was just her presence, her empathy, compassion and some good humour that helped me through that terrible day.

That day, I realized that we had a very special friendship. I also realized that she would go to the ends of the earth to help a friend and I had to be prepared to do the same for her if ever needed.

So how did we become such good friends? How did we move from acquaintances chatting at the end of a workday to spending time three days a week working out together for 13 years or more and being included in each other's group of friends? After all, there is almost a 20-year difference in our age.

One factor was that, whether running, walking, skiing or cycling, we were close in ability, which made it fun to have a training partner and it allowed us the time to slowly get to know each other much better.

We also motivated each other to get out and exercise. Even on days when I didn't feel like going, I always had to remember that Nicole was expecting me to be there at a certain time. Once out there, the exercise felt great.

I still smile when I think about the first time we exercised together. My wife Jaye worked at a downtown college, and Nicole was her manager of academic administration. On one of the days when I stopped at the college to meet Jaye for the drive home, she wasn't ready so, as I often did, I sat talking to Nicole, whose office was next to Jaye's. She asked what I was doing on the weekend and I replied that I was going cross-country skiing on Sunday. Nicole immediately asked if she could join me. I said yes as having company on the trails would be nice. The next day I got a call from Nicole asking what time we were skiing and wondering why I hadn't mentioned our ski outing to Jaye. The truth was I had expected something else would come up and I wouldn't hear from Nicole. I never made that mistake again. Chalk that up to learning that when Nicole says she is going to do something, she does it.

That first ski outing led to us planning the next and the next and the next, which grew to the three weekly exercise sessions that have continued for more than a decade.

I only recently learned that Jaye had told her sister that she believed those exercise sessions helped me maintain my mental health during more than 10 years as the primary caregiver and managing other caregivers as my wife's Amyotrophic lateral sclerosis (ALS) also known as Lou Gehrig's Disease progressed. On reflection, I would say it was a lot more than just the exercise. These were fixed points through the week when I knew I could depressurize, vent or just forget about things, let the conversation wander and enjoy a cup of coffee or a glass of wine before heading home to deal with the reality of Jaye's health struggles. Like Lucy in the Peanuts comic strip, with her Psychiatric Help booth, on many of our days together Nicole should have hung out a sign reading "The Doctor is in."

Trust very quickly became a keystone of our relationship. I was so comfortable talking to her. I would open up and tell her things that I had told very few people. I gave her the same opportunity to talk freely, knowing that whatever was said would never be shared inappropriately. Over the years, I have had friends who I avoided telling certain things that were mildly embarrassing or personal because they would seem to blurt them out to people I really didn't want to know. I have never had that worry with Nicole, which is quite liberating because no subject is off-limits.

It took me a lot of years to realize that during some of our walks, when Nicole was talking, it wasn't a conversation so much as an internal debate she was having to resolve some issue. When her words are spilling out and her emotions are running high, she uses what I like to think of as 'physical punctuation.' A hand will flash out and hit my arm, like an exclamation point. I doubt she even realizes it happens.

This friendship has grown to be so much more than just exercising together. Over the years, I feel that I have become a member of Nicole and Gavin's extended family. I have been invited to both of their daughters' weddings. I've been invited to many evenings around the fire and to what has been called Nicole's Christmas Eve dinner for her single friends.

We have just returned from a second European vacation, which ended with a cycle-and-cruise and included touring parts of the Netherlands and visiting several of Gavin's relatives. Again, I was treated like a family member.

Often, Nicole and I will have supper together after a workout when Gavin is working late shifts. It's more pleasant than each of us eating alone and is an opportunity to have things like lamb and fish that don't rate high among Gavin's favourites.

Nicole stepped in big time to help me when Jaye died. She went to the funeral home with me. She was my minder on the day we held the celebration of life, a touch on the arm or a word to keep me on track. She helped me clear out Jaye's clothing. She did whatever was required but most importantly, she was available whenever I needed to talk. Those things were crucial in helping me cope with the loss.

A wise woman told me at that time: "Don't turn down any invitation." I tried to live by that motto. Nicole and Gavin certainly did their part by making sure there were lots of invitations to keep me busy, especially those nights with friends around their fire pit.

I don't often think about what makes a great friendship or why two people develop a strong bond. Maybe I should spend more time thinking about it, as I am being forced to do while I write this chapter. Nicole has the knack of pushing me outside my comfort zone, with great delight I am sure.

When she first talked about this project and invited me to be part of it, I told her that writing wasn't my thing, never had been. But I never seriously considered declining because I knew that she would not accept 'no' as an answer and she would win in the end. At that point she hadn't told me I was the only male she had asked to participate. That came much later and was accompanied by a grin and a devilish glint in her eyes. Ratchet up the pressure!

When I think about Nicole and the traits she brings to a relationship the list rolls out easily. She is loving, compassionate, honest, loyal, enthusiastic, high energy, ambitious, confident, open and so much more.

Nicole cares deeply about family, friends and acquaintances, and about their well-being, both physical and mental. Sometimes I think she takes too much of the burden on her own shoulders but it is done with deep compassion and caring for others. Her compassion is not only directed at humans but at animals as well. Witness Ronan, the rescue hound, who is the official greeter when you arrive at Nicole and Gavin's. They had fostered Ronan and his brother Hogan. When it came time for Ronan to be placed in a permanent home, such a bond had developed between him and Nicole the only thing that made sense was him staying right there.

Honesty, at times brutal honesty, is something that Nicole doesn't shy away from. When you are the recipient, as I have been on several occasions, it is hard to think of this as tough love but that is exactly what it is. That honesty is not meant to hurt; it comes from a place of caring and the best of intentions so you had better go away and think about it and make changes — because Nicole doesn't suffer fools lightly.

The enthusiasm Nicole has for so many things and the energy she brings to that enthusiasm is contagious. It sometimes has me running to keep up but it keeps me feeling young.

In my group of friends most are women. Why is that? Why am I able to develop strong friendships with assertive, intelligent and confident women?

I grew up in a home with two sisters. Our parents worked hard to support us in every way but most important was our education. At that time, about 60 years ago, educational opportunities for women were dramatically different than they are now.

My older sister struggled for several years to get admitted to medical school. Watching that and hearing of the difficulties that both sisters faced simply because they were female was instrumental in me growing up with the attitude that if I couldn't tolerate how some people treated my sisters I would never treat any woman that same way. I believe that I have put that attitude into practice, and that is part of why I get along so well with so many women.

Stephanie, the personal trainer I have worked with for about five years, has in a short time become a good friend. During those years, as I recovered from a heart attack and torn tendons in my shoulder, Steph kept me laughing and enjoying the physical effort as she adapted workouts to deal with my health issues. She is a strong woman both physically and mentally, a great listener and has wisdom far beyond her years.

Marlene and I have been friends for more than 30 years. We met in Saskatoon when we worked for the same government department. Marlene is a woman who has never let a physical disability stop her from travelling the world. Early on, I asked her if I should offer to help her and she made it clear that if she needed help she would ask, and that has remained true over all these years. We have a close relationship with an easy ability to talk and laugh at just about anything.

Joanne is my sister-in-law. We met through Jaye and for many years we saw each other occasionally and talked on birthdays or at Christmas. After Jaye was diagnosed with ALS Joanne began to travel regularly to Edmonton and that is when we became friends. We stay in touch and have long phone calls every few weeks.

Each of these women and several others as well, I can reach out to when I need to talk. But I know the first person I will always turn to is Nicole.

Nicole recently used the term 'bedrock,' and I think that is an apt description of how I see her. For all the reasons I have written here, she is the solid base where I feel most comfortable and least vulnerable.

Nicole, I love you and I treasure our incredible friendship.

Ian McKay

I am a prairie boy born in Regina, Saskatchewan. I am a father of three adult boys.

I was a chemist in the brewing industry who, quite by accident, moved into financial management with two government departments. I have been retired for about 12 years and love it.

I work at staying fit by cycling, cross-country skiing, walking and strength workouts. I have had the same training partner for 13 or more years. The beauty of this long relationship is that we push each other to be out there three times a week, even on days that one of us is not motivated to exercise.

I have an eclectic group of friends who enjoy gathering for a glass of wine, dinner and wide-ranging conversations that can touch on almost any subject. This is the group that helps me feel way younger than my years.

Lifelong Allies

Kim Krushell

In life there are friends and then there are friends who turn into 'besties.' These are the friends who know everything about you, you spend time with and are loyal to each other through the ups and downs of life. You may not always get along and may at times lose touch with one another but when the chips are down, it is this friend you reach out to. I learned about this type of friendship by watching my mom and her best friend Carole. They met in 1968, in Hollywood, just as the idealistic peace-and-love movement took a dark turn with the assassination of Martin Luther King Jr. and then Robert F. Kennedy, and the escalation of the Vietnam War. What is truly amazing is that despite many life changes for both they stayed friends for 47 years until Carole passed away.

Growing up as an only child of divorced hippie Democratic parents who were a stark contrast to my conservative Republican grandparents, I got an early education on how to read a room, avoid conflict and be empathetic. I also learned at an early age that if I did not want to be alone with only adults for company I needed to make friends and put myself out there. Like my mom, I have had many friends but only a few close friends and one bestie, with whom I have been friends for almost 25 years: Nicole.

Nicole and I are in some ways opposites. She is incredibly energetic, organized and very driven. Her superpower is that when she is with you, she is always present in the moment. Her ability to unplug and focus on who she is with is truly a gift and is valued by her many friends. I met Nicole in 1999 when I joined a women's service organization, the Junior League of Edmonton (JLE), and Nicole was the organization's president. Nicole stood out to me as she was an excellent meeting chair, a good speaker and very effective at organizing and motivating members to complete tasks.

We did not interact much until the following year when I was recovering from surgery after the birth of my son and had, as a result, missed several meetings. Nicole was the person tasked with finding out if I was OK. Her understanding and friendship are what made me decide to stick with the women's organization. I'm glad I did because some of my closest friends today are either people I met or recruited to the JLE. We also got to work on some amazing community projects and fundraisers, and helped a lot of organizations in our community as a result. Sadly, the JLE is no longer operating but joining a service organization or a non-profit board is a great way to not only build friendships but also make a difference.

If you want to know everything about a person, get them involved in a political campaign! It was through politics that Nicole and I really got to know everything about each other. In a provincial election campaign in 2008 we were tasked with helping win a seat where our original candidate had to drop out. That candidate had name recognition, volunteers and money but the replacement candidate had none of these things. When I asked Nicole if she wanted to get involved she said yes. We truly bonded and became best friends during this trial by fire.

Nicole and I took on multiple roles in this campaign and forced our reluctant candidate to get out into the constituency and knock on doors. The opposing candidate had name recognition as he had served as an elected official so the odds of us winning were not good. In fact, the odds were so bad that our party did not put much effort into helping us win. During this crazy experience Nicole and I learned that we work well together in stressful, high-stakes situations and that we both loved the excitement of a political campaign.

Nicole is amazing at time management, scheduling and organizing, all key skills you need in campaigns. I had the campaign experience and we were both good at inspiring people to get involved and work hard. Through sheer grit we managed to put on a credible campaign and on election night it was a shocking upset when our candidate surprisingly won.

After that campaign the two of us got even more involved in politics over the years and at all levels of government. Eventually, at different times in our lives, we both ran for office and experienced what it's like to be a candidate. We both have endless campaign war stories, and we met and made friends with a lot of amazing people over the years. Today, sadly, politics is a lot more divisive but is still a way to connect with people and make new friends as well as learn about what goes on in a campaign and maybe consider running for elected office. Democracy does not work if we do not attract good people to run. Both of us experienced many highs and lows as well as intense stress throughout the years we were involved in politics but we also forged an unbreakable bond and shared meaningful life experiences on and off the campaign trail.

Another way to make lasting friendships is to travel with friends. We started travelling with Nicole and Gavin to celebrate our milestone wedding anniversaries. Nicole and Gavin are very experienced travellers and enjoy finding amazing travel deals, mapping out the travel itinerary, picking the Airbnbs and hotels, and planning the activities, while my husband and I are happy to go along for the ride.

I have many memories of our trips. One that stands out was Las Vegas, for our 25th wedding anniversary. Nicole and I had the glam squad show up to do our hair and makeup. We looked amazing until we got into the hired limo, which had no AC, and we started to melt, at which point, Nicole started to fan my face, hoping the makeup would, by some miracle, hold up until we made it to the Elvis chapel to renew our wedding vows.

Other memories from our trips to Europe include how excited I was to get to drive on the famous Autobahn, only to find out that our rental car could not go over 180 km/hour, if that. And the time the four of us were in Italy where we hired a chef, and learned how to make the most amazing Italian meal, which included homemade pasta paired with great wine. Or the time we discovered the rental car we ordered was too small to fit any of our luggage and we had quite the crazy challenge finding a large enough vehicle. (In large part due to the size of my well-stocked luggage!) My husband and I have discovered that travelling with our best friends makes the whole experience more enjoyable and provides shared memories that bring us closer.

Over the years Nicole and I have been there for the bittersweet moments, such as when our kids grew up and left home. There have also been moments of great joy, such as the weddings of Nicole and Gavin's daughters and the birth of their first grandson. We have also supported each other through the sudden and tragic loss of close loved ones and the devastation of seeing Alzheimer's take away people we love. We have supported each other through various health issues over the years and have been through a lot of challenging life experiences that have continued to strengthen our friendship.

We are soul sisters. When we are feeling overwhelmed, stressed, scared or just need company we are there for each other. Nicole is truly one of the few people that I let get behind the curtain, who I can be myself with. She understands that my childhood story has made it challenging at times for me to see myself in a positive way. This is something many women struggle with. Nicole and I have intentionally focused on working hard to break these negative patterns that many women are familiar with, by supporting one another to take risks and embrace change. Over the years the two of us have empowered each other and lifted each other up.

Just as I have had my struggles, Nicole has also faced some tough challenges. I have been the one who can connect in a way that Nicole will listen to and she often takes my advice. One time, Nicole was totally misreading her husband and ended up on my doorstep with her overnight bag. After talking it through, I began to realize that Nicole was overanalyzing the situation and reading way more into it than what was really happening. It turned out to be the classic Marge and Homer Simpson scenario and we still laugh about it today!

One touching and unexpected outcome of our friendship has been our moms becoming good friends. Whatever life throws at us, I know that Nicole and I will always be there for each other as we have a lifetime of shared experiences and memories, including the writing of this book. We plan to grow old gracefully, together.

Kim Krushell

Treefort Technologies
Co-Founder, EVP Information Security & HR

https://www.linkedin.com/in/kimkrushell/
https://treeforttech.com/

Throughout my life, friends have encouraged me to do things I'm not sure I would have been brave enough to do on my own, such as studying abroad as an American exchange student in Seoul, South Korea where I met my Canadian husband, Jay or getting into politics and being elected as an Edmonton city councillor.

Without encouragement from friends, I do not know if I would be living a whole new chapter of my life in tech. It's still a bit crazy to me how my husband and I took a big chance and co-founded Treefort Technologies. Today, Treefort is a leader in identity verification in Canada for compliance and identity fraud prevention.

I have learned there are many ways to connect, make new friends and challenge yourself, including doing my best to write a chapter in this book to honour my best friend Nicole.

More Than Family: The Deep Connection Between Mother and Daughter

Louise Guay

On my fridge, there is a magnet that reads: "There is nothing quite as precious as a daughter who is also a friend." From my perspective, no truer words have been written. When my daughter, our first child, was born at the St. Boniface Hospital on Nov. 23, 1964 it was one of the happiest days of my life.

As a young woman in the early 1950s I worked as a legal secretary and bookkeeper. There, I met and made lifetime friends. We were all legal secretaries in various offices at the Confederation Building. We gathered each workday for a coffee and a bagel, mostly to share the news of new clients, new hires and office relationships. One of the lawyers said he wished he could be a fly on the wall during our morning 'briefings.' It really was the original version of Peyton Place!

I maintained contact with these friends and when I returned to Winnipeg for family events, we would find an evening to get together to share old stories and get caught up on each other's lives. We were always able to restart the conversation where we had last left off even if years had passed.

When I married, our circle of friends was plentiful. So plentiful that my sister told me years later that she was envious of all of the parties and events we were invited to. I could not write a friendship story without acknowledging our dearest friends Lee and George, who we'd known since our school days. In our retirement years they wintered with us in Arizona.

Beryl was one of my favourite friends. She was smart, witty and very much a believer in women's rights who likely influenced my adolescent daughter. We spent many good times at the summer cabin with our children. We would play Scrabble late into the night and in the mornings would get our spouses to take the kids to the lake so we could go back to bed for a couple of hours, having been sleep-deprived. I am grateful for all of the good times we shared as she passed away at a very young age from cancer. So, words of wisdom: enjoy your friendships as you never know what the future will hold. To this day, I maintain a friendship with her two adult children.

Two other very special friends were Carmen and Ben. They never had children of their own, so our children became their children. They were invited to and attended every important family event: birthdays, anniversaries, weddings, baptisms, funerals and other special events. Carmen was a real fashionista and was thrilled when she was invited to shop for our only daughter's wedding dress. Nicole found a beautiful gown with a long train that was elegant and classy.

When we moved to Edmonton in the early '70s we began a new life and made many new friends, some of them through our two boys' sporting activities. Many of my husband Andy's customers also become our friends, like Ackram and his beautiful wife Nancy. Ackram is like a son to us – that is how close our friendship has grown over the years. Each winter they would travel to Arizona to spend some time in the sun. Playing Dominoes was one of our favourite games and we had to play until Nancy won. Having fun is such an important part of spending time with friends.

Another special couple we met through Andy's work were Marcel and his wife Suzanne. We continued to see them weekly even after retirement. I am so grateful for their continuing friendship because, at this stage of my life, many friends have passed. Fortunately, memories last forever.

Of all my friendships, the most special is the one with my only daughter, Nicole.

It has been amazing to see my daughter grow and become the person she is. Nicole is very caring and generous, always prepared to help when needed. Her greatest gift to me has been her friendship!

In the fall of 2011, Nicole took me on a mother-and-daughter trip to England, Ireland, Scotland and Wales. We spent three weeks touring and learned so much about these countries. One of the highlights was the high tea she booked for us at the Ritz London. It was like we were royalty in a beautiful heritage building. Each year, she invites me as her guest to a fundraiser that has a high tea, a reminder of that first one in London, England.

Nicole came to see us in Arizona every year we wintered 'down south,' spending a week enjoying the sun and our company. During our travels and time together, I learned a lot about who she is as a woman and the things that are important to her, including her goals and dreams. She has worked hard to attain all that she has achieved in her life. She has always invited everyone to join her in special projects or events, like her run as a candidate in our municipal election and now this friendship anthology. My goodness – the yellow stickers she uses to remind her of her to-dos and to-gets must have multiplied a hundredfold since the start of this anthology project.

To become mother-and-daughter friends, above all else, you must respect one another.

Over the years, when various issues needed to be discussed, sometimes there would be a difference of opinion. But being able to have different opinions and still be in a relationship is important. In our discussions, sometimes she would be right; at times I was right; and often we found we shared a common position. The outcome was always the same – we remained friends. We have always been able to laugh and cry together in times of great joy and terrible grief. We have always supported one another, in any situation, because of the deep understanding we have about each other.

As a friend, I trust Nicole completely. I am not afraid to discuss my problems and seek her assistance. I can be myself in the moment. I like being with her. I like seeing and hearing about all the projects she is doing. I like to hear about her new clients at work. I have always encouraged her to fulfil her dreams. I like her friends and some of them have become my friends too.

When Nicole became a mother the bond between us became stronger. I wanted to share her joy in having children. My husband and I were included in every special occasion with her children and actively participated in their lives. She was, and is, an awesome mother. Caring, giving, helping, doing all that her children needed, putting them first and supporting them to achieve their goals in life. And as a result of her organizational skills she was still able to carve out time to cross-stitch with me or a friend in the evening, to scrapbook, bake a special birthday cake or get out for a quick run to clear her head and get some fresh air.

I am fortunate to have had the blessing of a mother-daughter relationship over the years. My sincere hope is that every mother can become a friend to their daughter. And that every daughter makes it a priority to become a friend to their mother. I am forever grateful and hope our special friendship journey continues for many more years.

Louise Guay

https://www.facebook.com/profile.php?id=100000943365508

I am a mother of three adult children, a grandmother to three young women and a great-grandmother. I have been married to my husband Andy for 61 years. My family and friends are important to me and have supported me through many challenging times in my life.

Some of my most memorable times were spent at our cabin on Lake Winnipeg. My husband's job allowed us to travel to many places in the U.S. and we wintered there for many years. I was an avid cross-stitcher. Today I am a caregiver to my husband. I enjoy following politics, especially U.S. politics.

My advice to those looking for a good friend is to follow your heart. Good friends are the ones who you can trust, respect and rely on in good and bad times. For my family and friends my motto has been and will always be: My love is unconditional.

Just say yes!

Nancy Beasley Hosker

We were camping, Nicole, our husbands and I; they were in a pup tent for two and we were in our comfy trailer. I had insisted they use the mattress from the extra bed in our trailer as Nicole and Gavin preferred the tent. She reluctantly agreed — they really did like roughing it. Rain was forecast so they put a tarp under the tent. I added a shield tarp tied to a tree to keep some of the rain at bay.

It stormed most of the night, with heavy rain, high winds and lightning. The next morning, I stepped out of the trailer to see how our campers had fared. "Well," said Nicole, unzipping the tent into a brilliant morning at the provincial campground not far from home. "We're dry, but your mattress is soaked." We all laughed when we realized that the reason for the soaking was that my brilliant idea to shield them had actually created a torrent of rain that turned into a stream running through the inside of their tent.

With that laughter, our sister-friendship was cemented: if you can laugh while wringing out the only extra clothes you brought camping and NOT blame your friend for sending teeming water your way, you can likely laugh at anything.

As I reflect on moments like this, with Nicole, some of the contributing authors to this anthology and the women with whom I have shared my life, I realize that the ties that bind us are trust, commitment, integrity, caring and giving. These are the attributes of my women friends with whom I have never felt the need to compete. They celebrate my successes, lift me up when I stumble, hold my hand in moments of sorrow and laugh, laugh, laugh when happiness or just silliness, prevails. These are my learnings from years of friendship lessons.

Another lesson that took many years to learn is that I should trust my first instinct in pretty much everything, especially when it comes to trusting a new acquaintance. There have been times when I haven't done so and in most of those cases, I have lived with regret — either that I should have accepted the offer of friendship and nurtured it but instead let a wonderful friendship opportunity pass me by or I should have rejected it since, in the end, the acceptance led to disappointment and pain. These are lessons that help to build our character, develop stronger instincts and enable us to truly trust when we cross paths with women with whom lifelong friendships may blossom.

I met my friend Carrie at age six in ballet class. It's so much easier to make friends as a child, even when you don't go to the same school. Every child you meet at six is your friend. Keeping those friends into adulthood is another matter. Yet here we are 60 years later, still connected in our hearts even though we have been separated by vast distances for nearly 50 of those years.

When I moved from Ottawa to London, Ont. at 15 years old, I gave her a tiny book about friendship, the title of which I remember all these years later: A Friend is a Present You Give Yourself. I cherish the gift of Carrie's friendship. Sometimes one of us will call or text at just the right moment, when the other may be struggling or wanting to share some special moment of joy. When I think of these times, I wonder whether intuition is perhaps strongest when the ties that bind are strongest, when we and our friends have endured countless joys and hardships together. There have also been times when I felt I was not as attentive to our friendship as I should have been and have lived with regret, another learning opportunity to try not to let that happen again.

Forgiveness, for these moments of lapsed friendship or other emotional hurt, is a gift my friends possess. I often think that we judge ourselves more harshly than those who love us and have found that the best way to forgive ourselves is to ask our friends to forgive us for those trespasses. This takes courage as we have to admit we have erred and face potential backlash if forgiveness isn't forthcoming. What surprises me is that often the burdens I may carry in my heart have not even occurred to my dear friends — they simply don't judge. And if they have harboured some hurt as a result of my actions, opening myself up to forgiveness mends the rift between us. Lifting that burden of guilt clears our hearts and minds for connectedness in the future.

Developing friendships as an adult is much more difficult. We carry with us many relationship experiences, both good and bad. It's much easier for a six-year-old to say "Want to be my friend?" than it is for an adult. But if we persevere, we may succeed: making friends with a work colleague, a fellow volunteer, a fellow parent or someone we run into regularly at the gym, a local store or a coffee shop. Clearly, it's a risk to say to an acquaintance "Want to be my friend?" but an invitation to meet for coffee, go for a walk, have a shopping day together or grab lunch can be worth it to earn a friend-for-life.

Since those early life friendships, many women have come into my life, some staying and some passing through. Regardless of the length of time, the gifts of those friendships are etched in my heart.

Some of these etchings hurt terribly. One of our very dear friends passed during the lost COVID years. Denise was an integral member of my village, part of my soul. We were godmothers to each other's youngest children; we laughed, cried, crafted, camped and shared more than a couple of glasses of wine. My heart aches for the loss of this soul-sister but also rejoices that we had many years together. Do not be afraid to love your friend, even in the face of potential loss.

Denise was also part of Nicole's circle, along with other members of this amazing group of writers who are sharing their stories. Each of us has joined her circle from different paths but we share one very strong bond — the unquestioning friendship Nicole offers to each of us.

Other etchings came when I made friends at work, some when I started my career as a journalist. In those early years, my workmates didn't compete but rather supported each other. I am still good friends with two of these women, though much time and distance separates us.

Still more connections came as a mom, with other moms through our children. Some of them would become lifelong friends in their own right: our children have grown and many have gone their separate ways but the bonds with these women are now unbreakable. Today we camp together, play board or outdoor games, have dinners or just hang out.

My relationship with my adult children is shifting from parent-child to friendship and I count my sister and her spouse among my very best friends. These family relationships are critical to my peace and happiness.

Maintaining these friendships requires commitment, energy and time, but they are more than worth the effort. Nicole and I met nearly 20 years ago when our daughters were in Girl Guides. At that time, we were both leaders, mothers, professionals and occasionally adults in our own right. With three children of my own, then under 16, and she with two, we didn't connect as friends but more as volunteers.

Fast forward a few years as I walked into a meeting of people supporting a local candidate for the next election. Nicole was there as a volunteer for the candidate, welcoming all who entered. I would later learn that Nicole had been involved in politics for most of her adult life.

"You may not remember," she said, "but we met as Guide leaders. We're looking for new board members. How about I put your name down?"

Thus began an acquaintance that grew into today's sister-friendship. In a flash, we were tied at the hip, in friendship and supporting local candidates until Nicole was ready to embark on her own campaign.

I know that whenever Nicole says, "I have an idea!" I'm in for a new adventure, whether it's getting in my steps door-knocking or on the phone to support her as a local candidate, enjoying summer or winter fires around the backyard firepit, meeting for coffee, going for a walk, girls' night out for dinner and, yes, wine, dinner at home with spouses and friends, camping, attending political events or, the latest venture, enjoying a bike-and-barge trip in the Netherlands. I'm not really a cyclist but Nicole was her exuberant self about promoting the benefits of biking and the joy of trips on a bike abroad. Who knew I could cycle more than 300 km in six days!

Nicole doesn't leave a lot of room for you to say no when she has an idea percolating and she wants you involved. Because of this, I have enjoyed many new experiences by joining her in adventures over the years. And Nicole, with her gentle caring and sometimes less gentle cajoling, helped to drag me out of a brief shadow of darkness to truly re-engage with life. This is her 'Just say yes!' attitude. I have also been her anchor when she has struggled with what life has sent her way — with family, friends, work or just herself.

Our husbands have also developed their own friendship, conveniently since we often like to include them in our adventures.

And many of the women in Nicole's circle have become part of my circle.

I think a true test of friendship is that friends don't always agree, but can respectfully disagree, have a discussion and then move on. Sadly, not all people are able to make the distinction between opinion and fact, to accept that theirs may not be the only point of view. Where Nicole has strengthened my ability to say yes, I have given her opportunities to consider an alternate point of view. Our friendship strengthens as much through times of consensus as it does through times of dissension, though in reality, we enjoy more of the former.

We can do this as we have a shared gift of being able to create a safe space for friends to tell their truths and to hear observations about their behaviours, actions or reactions about which they may be unaware. Nicole is very good at listening, observing and then expressing her observations with an honest and clear voice, and always with the voice of caring. These quiet critical conversations would be around our personal lives, our professional lives or even our volunteer lives. The gems of truth Nicole has provided have stretched my ability to think before I speak and speak before I act…most of the time.

She has helped me step outside of my comfort zone and face new challenges even in the face of potential failure. This encouragement has, I think, helped make me a better person and strengthened my sense of self-worth, a definite plus to having good friends.

One such adventure involved a vision of what she wanted for her daughter's engagement party. She'd been carrying a newspaper clipping in her wallet for years, a recipe for Croquembouche. I searched the internet to learn that this was essentially a small mountain of homemade mini cream puffs finished with tiny wisps of caramel-like thread. "Have you mistaken me for my daughter, the professional baker?" I asked. "No," was the response. "I just know I've always wanted this and I know you can make it happen." How do you say no to a friend who either has that much faith in you or is desperate? I choose to believe it's faith.

Never one to shrink from a challenge, I figured out how to make this somewhat exotic-sounding pastry, the most difficult parts of which were the wispy, caramel string decorations. The recipe says 30 minutes of prep time. It's a lie. After two hours of prepping and baking the pastry, another hour of making the vanilla filling, and then injecting it into the puffs, I was ready to build the mountain. After another two hours of figuring out how to make caramel string, Nicole's vision was a reality. Someday I may attempt to make it again — or ask Nicole to give it a try.

Then came the request to bake a wedding cake for one of her daughters. To be clear, I am a writer — not a baker — though I make a mean butter tart and apple pie. In keeping with the 'Just say yes!' theme, I said yes. "She wants a naked cake," I was informed. While that brought interesting pictures to mind, I sought the advice of my Red-Seal-baker daughter. It wasn't nearly as risqué as I originally thought.

Advice in hand, I baked six round pink champagne cakes of different sizes and froze them in preparation for icing. Note to all, before you freeze cakes, put them in stacks of two on a cardboard round and insert dowels of the same height to create holes for the supports needed between double layers. I missed that step, which turned the wedding cake assembly into more of a strongman project. There we were, Nicole and I, at the table on my back deck (it was during the COVID years so we couldn't be inside together and had to wear masks), with thoroughly frozen round cakes into which we were attempting to hammer, with all of our might, supporting dowels. I have never laughed so hard over cake and icing as I did that day. My daughter also laughed when she heard of our antics: I was glad to share the hilarity of our mistakes.

The wedding cake looked beautiful, in all its nakedness, and the bride and groom were happy. In the meantime, through both tasks, I learned more new skills and had a blast, all thanks to Nicole's adage, "Just say yes!"

Oscar Wilde wrote: "With age comes wisdom, but sometimes age comes alone." I believe Nicole and, by extension, we women in our circles, embody both ideas. Age and experience, a willingness to learn and to accept alternate opinions, and the ability to freely share our authentic selves lead us to a wisdom that we can enjoy as time passes. Sadly, we are all human and may not see those great gifts all the time: we have times when we simply age and miss opportunities for wisdom.

It is during those times of missed opportunities that we need our truest friends by our side. We go through the motions of each day unaware of the experiences that pass us by. Sometimes fear holds us back; at other times, it may be sadness, or worse, depression. When we can work our way back to ourselves, alone or with the help of those we love, those lost times can provide a type of wisdom of their own. And the real learning is that when we have a village, we are never really alone.

Now, as a 66-year-old woman who loves life and is not afraid to say so, I cherish the friends in my life, those I share with Nicole and those I have in other parts of my life. They all bring me joy, support and love. I hope they feel the same coming from me. I will never regret taking the risk to make a new friend, even now, as the power of friendship can only make us each a better person.

We are blessed with amazing lives. What a great gift we have, this deep and abiding friendship that allows us to share our ideas, our thoughts and even our differences, and come out stronger for it. Thank you, Nicole, and all the incredible women friends in my circle, for enriching my life.

Nancy Beasley Hosker

I am a mother of three, a grandmother of two and have been married for 36 years. As an experienced journalist, writer, editor and public affairs advisor I focus on providing high-quality work, always striving to deliver more than expected.

I value relationships: family and friends always come first. I have learned to trust my instincts, which has helped me build stronger relationships with those who are part of my circle and let go of people who do not share my values.

My circle includes women of all ages - my longest-time friend of 60 years to one of less than one year - women who have supported, influenced or shared their lives with me. As a close friend of the primary author, I am sharing my experiences through this unique anthology with the hope that these stories will bring light to readers around the world.

A Blend of Shared Experiences and Laughter

Shannon Brice

If asked to define the term friendship, there would be many different answers based on a person's values. One basic definition is building strong, supportive relationships with people you can trust. This lays the foundation but there are many different components and attributes individuals may value when forming friendships. One of the most difficult things is to be honest and authentic to yourself and your friends. Sometimes honesty may lead to hurt feelings but being authentic and honest allows you to put aside any façade and create genuine friendships. I am very lucky the friendships that have sustained me throughout my life have been with authentic individuals. This has allowed me to share a few of my favourite friendship stories here.

Sharing similar values usually draws people together early in their relationship. As friendship develops, those shared values help to build a sense of trust and loyalty. But sharing similar values does not mean always sharing the same opinion or agreeing on everything. Having differing opinions, perspectives or views is crucial to continuing to grow and seeing things from a different point of view. Unfortunately in today's world everyone seems to be tentative about their perspective if it is different, goes against the latest societal values or isn't the same as your friends' and colleagues' beliefs.

It doesn't matter what job you have — you must be able to connect with your colleagues to be part of the team. I was extremely fortunate that I collaborated with great fellow educators over the years but there was a special group that turned into friends. The turning point from colleague to friendship was when we realized that we all had shared values but very differing opinions, which was OK. There was a feeling of security being in an environment that allowed for free discussion on differing points of view, playing devil's advocate and sometimes saying something that might be inappropriate but always knowing that the discussions were open and never went outside the four walls. It was reassuring to know that your point of view was heard and valued.

Agreeing to disagree is OK. Not everyone is always going to agree, but the ability to be open to diverse perspectives leads to individual growth and learning. During each school year, as a member of the faculty, I spent more time with these people than anybody else and knew that even though we sometimes had differing opinions, there was no judgment. I look back at our shared lunches, meetings, social get-togethers, practical jokes, laughing and daily interactions, and realize that the number one thing I miss now that I am retired is the people I worked with and called my friends.

New or old, mundane or extraordinary, every shared experience creates opportunities that bring people closer together. Creating those memories lays the foundation for any friendship. Once upon a time, five girls who became friends in high school developed an unbreakable bond that has lasted throughout the years. As we grew up we ventured into various careers: two became teachers, one worked in hospitality, one became a hair stylist and one worked in their family business.

Despite our busy and changing lives, as adults, we always made time to get together once a month for dinner. These gatherings were held at everyone's house on a rotating basis. In the early years of entertaining, this proved to be a challenge as everyone wanted to cook a great meal and ensure the perfect evening as the hostess. As you can imagine, it didn't always go as planned. Here's one of our stories.

One of the girls had just moved into a new house and it was her turn for dinner. She cleaned and cooked for the entire day, looking forward to a perfect evening. We arrived and had drinks and appetizers as we began to talk about what was going on in our lives. Things were going great and it was time for the big moment — dinner. The table was laid to perfection, the timing of the meal was perfect and everything was ready at the same time (something I am still working on to this day). As everyone helped to get the food to the table, talking and laughing, we all forgot to watch the dog. Before we knew it, the perfectly cooked pork roast was in the dog's mouth and five adults were on the chase to try to save the main course. It was like an Olympic event of hurdles, sprinting and long jumping before we retrieved what was left of the roast. Some people might have been mortified, but we all laughed, sat down and ate what was left for dinner.

These dinners may not have always been perfect but spending time together reminiscing, sharing stories from our different careers and catching up on the latest happenings in everyone's lives are the things we now remember.

As time moved on, lives changed: two moved to new cities, two started their families and everyday life became all-consuming. As we approached our 40th birthdays, the idea of a major reunion began to form. We decided to celebrate in Las Vegas, a place that provided a variety of things to do. The three days were spent gambling, going to shows, eating at a rooftop restaurant, reminiscing and lots of laughter. Fast forward 10 years and we decided to celebrate our 50th birthdays in Banff, a retreat in the mountains that would be much quieter than the trip to Vegas. We rented a cabin and spent the first night catching up on what was happening in everyone's lives. How were the kids? How were everyone's jobs going? How were everyone's parents? The discussions were endless. Laughter filled the cabin as we recalled wild escapades, from high school to the Vegas trip, promising one another that no matter where our lives led us, we would always find a way to celebrate our friendships together.

My key requirement of friendship is the ability to laugh together. Whether laughing at a mutually shared experience, each other or oneself, it builds the foundation that creates an environment of comfort and a positive shared memory. People who laugh together become closer and connect on a deeper level, which allows them to support each other when faced with challenges and adversity.

Friendships often find their roots in unexpected places. My friendship with Nicole began when we were teenagers working at the local swimming pool and attending our first years of university. I remember that Nicole was fun and liked to laugh but was also a bit scary. To this day, she does not hold back with her thoughts or opinions and that is one of the things that I have grown to love and appreciate. As we shared laughter during coffee breaks at work or late-night caffeine sessions while studying at school we began to find common interests. (By the way, she used to drag me to those study sessions and I am not sure I ever thanked her — better late than never — thank you.)

As our friendship grew we decided to take a trip to Mexico. This was the first time I had travelled outside Canada so I had grand expectations of fun, sun, beautiful beaches, great food and laughter. This was also the late 1980s when tanning was all the rage and baby oil was the sunscreen of choice. Most people would take it slow and build a base but with only two weeks in Mexico we dove right in for the perfect suntan. Lounging on the beach, swimming in the ocean and relaxing and enjoying ourselves soon turned to disaster. Despite using sunscreen (probably oil), Nicole ended up with a serious sunburn. This was not a regular sunburn where your skin gets a little pink and then turns into a tan; this was full-on RED on every part of her body. Fast forward to the later evening when Nicole comes out of the bathroom holding a towel to cover her and I didn't even recognize her — covered from head to toe in an entire jar of Noxzema.

Between the sunburn and the Noxzema we didn't need any lights as the glow coming off her body lit the entire room. It was a rough night since she couldn't lay on any part of her body without pain and she was suffering from sunstroke. I have a photo of that Noxzema-covered body but have sworn to never show anybody. Nicole's sunburn was bad, but she didn't let it deter her from continuing to have fun. That was my night to take care of my friend but she paid me back tenfold with my bout of food poisoning a couple of days later. Nothing shows true friendship more than holding your friend's hair back when they're throwing up, losing my entire dinner not once, but twice.

Those were two awful nights for both of us but what made the sunburn and food poisoning bearable was the fact that the next morning we laughed about our prior evenings' events. Our friendship trip to Mexico was a blend of sun-fun-laughter and unexpected challenges. From laughter on the beach to caring for each other during tough moments, the experience brought us closer and created lasting memories. In the end, sunburns and food poisoning became part of our shared friendship story, proof that even horrific experiences can create laughter and faithful friends.

One final thought: Many people view longevity as the true test of friendship, growing and adapting to changes throughout the years. In my experience, not all friendships last for years. We lose touch with friends when they move, change jobs or develop new interests we don't share. Since retiring, I have had the opportunity to reflect and one thing I have realized is that we cannot control time. We need to cherish all memories and stories — from past friendships, present friends and future friends we haven't yet met.

Shannon Brice

I was born in Saskatoon and raised in Sherwood Park. Growing up in a small community gave me the opportunity to develop meaningful relationships with neighbours, the chance to be involved and supported, and make friends, many of whom remain close to this day.

I recently retired from a fulfilling 33 years as a teacher. I was involved with coaching and mentoring students in a variety of different ways. My journey as a teacher began at the local swimming pool and eventually led to an education degree from the University of Alberta which then allowed me the privilege of teaching physical education and social studies at the high school level.

In addition to teaching, I cherish the moments spent with family and friends. Having the opportunity to travel with family, friends, on my own and on school trips allowed me to explore new places, see new cultures and create a desire to continue to develop further memories and experiences. I'm eager to plan my next journey, whether it be a weekend or a new country never visited. All my past travels have built my life so far with meaningful experiences, friendships and a desire to continue to travel.

Creating Close Friendships
Through Safe Space

Stephanie Boyd

The deepest friendships in life are the ones where the foundation is built from a judgment-free, trusting, respectful space where you can 100 percent be your authentic self. You can be the best or worst version of yourself and know that you're still loved by your closest friends. Having these relationships where it's safe to embrace and trust your authentic self allows you to go into the world more open-hearted and in tune with what and who you want in your life. You are more likely to attract authenticity or encourage people to embrace their genuine nature if you're ruthlessly yourself. The more in tune you are with yourself the more likely you are to get what you really want from life, including meaningful friendships.

I was fortunate that I developed my now-longest friendship at a very young age. He and a few other close friends in my youth helped me realize what being and having a true friend means. When you've known someone from the age of five until your current age you get to see them through a lot of different stages in life. You don't always get along and sometimes you even take breaks from one another but at the end of the day you always reconnect stronger and more in tune with yourself and who that other person is. These are the friends with whom I have had some of my most cherished, funniest and most pivotal moments.

We have seen one another through positive things like engagements and marriages as well as overcoming trauma to become more peaceful people. We have also had conversations or experiences that feel like they connect us as soulmates. Even better, we've conquered some horrible things in our lives like abusive relationships, bad friendships, family distress, depression, anxiety and stressful career changes.

My true friends are straight up with me no matter what. They're people who express their thoughts and feelings, being 100-percent honest with me even when I sometimes don't want to hear it. At the end of the day we always come back to one another to reflect on what has happened, positive or negative, to celebrate or in some cases learn how we could have been a better support for one another. Ultimately these types of conversations can only be had because of the safety we create in one another.

My closest friends are the ones I can talk to about anything — and I mean, anything — and in the way I need to express it within that moment, and vice versa. How or what is said is never judged and there is no need to hold back. I can fully be my goofy, sassy, dark-humoured, sometimes anxiety-ridden, depressed self and I know there is a safe space held for me no matter what the circumstance is.

Because I was lucky enough to have safe, meaningful friendships from such a young age, I believe it encouraged me to look for more of those friendships as an adult and it pushed me toward a career where I could meaningfully connect with other people. This brings me to how Nicole and I met. I've been a personal trainer for nearly 12 years and Nicole is one of the lovely individuals I've been blessed to meet on this journey through life. Although we still consistently train each week, the connection quickly surpassed that of a working relationship.

Inside and outside of sessions, Nicole and I have free-flowing conversations, discussing anything and everything, not just the surface stuff that you get out of most people. There are no masks you have to peel away. I don't have to try to decipher the words leaving her mouth and this has made it very easy for me to just be myself and freely express my inner world. Nicole doesn't hide who she is, which encouraged me to also show up authentically in our friendship.

Nicole has quite a sense of humour that allows us to banter and keep things entertaining while we go through our training sessions: "Are you sure you said four sets? I think you said two," she'd insist, knowing full well I said four sets. Or during one of our virtual workouts she'd get too hot, leave to go into the laundry room and come out wearing her husband's underwear to finish the rest of the workout. This friendship truly means a lot to me as we frequently align in our thought patterns, humour and things we enjoy in life. I know I will always have a truth-speaking, to-the-point, hilarious cheerleader in my life with Nicole around.

I strongly believe that accumulating meaningful friendships requires that both people consistently hold a safe space for the people in their lives. If there is a foundation of safety, then people are more likely to be themselves, which leads to connecting with people you truly align with. Once that happens these friendships will be everlasting. You know that you can get through anything with these individuals and you would do anything for them without hesitation, just as you know they would do the same for you.

Stephanie Boyd

Limitless Body Design
Personal Training Specialist

https://www.linkedin.com/in/steph-boyd-154aa7280/

I am a daughter, friend and coach in the health and fitness industry. I love spending time with friends and family, hiking, skiing, travelling, working out and dancing. I love adventure and enjoy learning about humans' inner psyche.

In my relationships I've always tried to approach people with an authentic open heart and willingness to listen to their thoughts, concerns and goals without judgment. As a result, people open up more and express deeper feelings, fears, excitements, plans or anything lingering in their minds and bodies. If this level of openness and love is the overall theme with the people around you, then this is the foundation for long-lasting, meaningful friendships. As a result, the friendships I've accumulated over the years are symbiotically deep-rooted.

I hope to convey in this anthology that the basis of any deep relationship is authenticity expressed in a safe space.

A Legacy of Love: Lessons from Extraordinary Women

Tracy Allen

Woman. The two-syllable word suggests someone who is soft, gentle and nurturing. But it can also mean someone who has spirit, immutable strength or pure, unfettered power. In her element, a woman can be a formidable creature: resilient, mentally sharp and quick-witted yet still warm and welcoming.

In some relationships, a woman plays a supporting role. In others, she is a fully engaged circus master juggling multiple fires, wild animals and competing priorities at home and work. A well-balanced woman can do it all and do it well. It can be intimidating to be in their presence because they are mesmerizing: I know because I have been privileged to be in the light of three of these dazzling creatures during my lifetime.

One is my mother, the other is my friend Nicole, but the first was my grandmother. The lessons I learned from them helped me understand the type of woman I should aspire to be and the kind of relationships I needed to create in order to have a joyful, compassionate life.

My parents divorced when I was just seven and I went to live with my father and later my stepmother. The divorce was bitter and emotionally devastating. I felt abandoned and alone after my mother left — and my father and his new wife refused to let me see her. I didn't reconnect with my mother until I was in my mid-30s.

Luckily I had my paternal grandmother, Ella Allen. She became my teacher, cheerleader and protector. She wasn't only my moral compass, she was the builder who picked up the broken pieces of my young life.

Growing up, I observed all the hard work she put into keeping her children and by extension, their families, close. She was the matriarch of our family and everything revolved around her. Our aunts, uncles, cousins and honorary family members celebrated every birthday, wedding, anniversary and holiday together. That meant I was lucky enough to grow up close to all my cousins. We spent every summer playing baseball, tag and countless other games on her front lawn. She was Grandma Allen to us and every other kid in town, and a stranger to none.

Ella Allen was a remarkable woman. She gave to all of us but paid special attention to the kids who didn't have grandmothers. She was a social butterfly and knew everyone in town. She always had a cookie and a kind word or hug, whether you were family or not. Allen Street — yes, the street was named after our family — was idyllic. A short tree-lined street that ended at a beautiful maple forest. A childhood fantasy land.

She spent winters knitting socks and blankets for those needing support and hosted countless quilting bees in her small living room with members of her church group. But what Grandma loved most was baking and cooking. She was always in her tiny kitchen baking cookies, pies, cakes and squares or making some of her famous stews or soups for a friend who was ill. I have never seen anyone give so freely of herself, with such pure joy, expecting nothing in return.

My grandmother balanced every aspect of what it is to be a wife, mother, grandmother and friend. In her world, family always came first but she was also a woman of faith who worked as hard to better her community and the lives of others as she did her own. My grandmother was funny and feisty, but humble, and communicated her emotion through the most beautiful, soft blue eyes. I was lucky to have grown up in her shadow and I hope one day to create half the lasting memories with my own family that she made with me. I gauge everything, at this point in my life against her and what I believe she would do. But I have to admit, she did it with far more charm and style than I ever could.

With my friends and grandmother, I was a smart, happy person growing up. At home, I had to endure violence and abuse at the hands of my stepmother. Things got so bad, I moved in with my grandmother when I was 15. Thanks to this incredible woman I lived safely, protected by her love until the day I graduated high school. In her home, I never wanted for anything.

The life I have today is a result of my grandmother's love and support. No one invested in me the way she did. Her values taught me to temper my anger and some violent tendencies that I learned when surrounded by violence and abuse at home. Although she passed away 21 years ago, in her honour I try to live my life the way she lived hers.

When my mother and I reconnected when I was in my mid-30s I learned many things as we bonded. One of the most important was discovering and embracing my First Nation ancestry. Growing up I didn't even know I had First Nation ancestors. My stepmother had apparently said, "There would be no Indians in HER family." It was because of my mother's strength and her willingness to share her own pain that she was able to take mine. Thanks to her selflessness, I persevered. Contrary to all of my stepmother's efforts, I am extremely proud of my Mohawk heritage. I survived all of her attacks because I am Mohawk. I am powerful because I am descended from warriors.

Unlike western, colonial hierarchies, in the world of Haudenosaunee people, Mohawk women are the leaders. They are clan mothers who make all of the decisions for their clan and community. It was women, not men, who determined the role each clan member would play in the long house. Though Mohawk men have long been venerated as fearsome warriors most people don't know that women were warriors, too.

When I look back on my life, I realize I have come full circle. I have always held a special place in my heart for those less fortunate, those who have been wronged, a champion for the protection of animals and the environment. But I cannot overstate the importance of learning life lessons at the feet of our elders.

One life lesson I have learned: trust your instincts. Listen. Trust in yourself. You know innately what is right and what is wrong. You know who deserves your love and you know who doesn't. It is our children who need all of the love, knowledge and wisdom we have to share as mothers and fathers. I am 54 and no matter how old I am I always find peace in my mother's voice. She gives me strength. I seek her out when I have a bad day because I know I have her unwavering love and support — her unconditional love.

As is the case in many families who experience trauma, my sisters and I grew apart. I will always love them and appreciate them for the women they are today but unhealthy relationships force you to relive trauma, and my sisters' inexcusable behaviour toward our mother is something I simply cannot tolerate. Accepting that they could no longer be in my life was a heart-breaking realization but it taught me another hard life lesson: value yourself. Put yourself first. Only by valuing yourself can you instil the same in others. Never hold on to traumatic or hurtful relationships; not even relationships with family.

Regardless of the complex history I have with members of my family, I pride myself on being able to maintain strong personal relationships. But they don't come easy. They require effort and a lot of hard work. They also require self-reflection and a commitment to growth and inner truth no matter how dark or terrifying. By acknowledging and accepting my childhood traumas and my flaws I have learned how to be open and vulnerable, how to make space for new, healthy relationships. I have learned how to navigate conflict — those who know me best say I thrive on it — but I see conflict as an opportunity for personal growth because I always learn something about myself. I also see navigating conflict as a way to achieve balance because balance comes with hard choices.

The relationships and bonds I foster and cherish today are all based on love, shared values and mutual respect. They centre on acceptance and reinforce a quiet sense of calm and maturity. I share these bonds with my husband, our daughter and her family, and an unbelievably tight-knit group of friends who, by virtue of our shared values and respect, are extensions of our immediate family.

These relationships keep me grounded and I hold them all close to my heart. I protect them because to me they are priceless. Before reaching middle age, I experienced decades of pain, hurt and doubt. The years between 20 and 40 were difficult, steeped in a host of bad decisions. I learned so much in those years.

I firmly believe, as women, we don't truly come into our own until our mid- to late-30s. It takes years of personal experience to find your voice and embrace who you are as a person, woman, wife and mother. It also takes strength to stand behind your values and beliefs, no matter how different or unpopular they may be. It's important to surround yourself with positive role models who have no personal agenda but to connect with like-minded women. Women who support women from a place of inner strength are all you need.

This brings me, finally, to my meeting with Nicole, this anthology's creator, a woman who is a mentor, supporter and one of the most important relationships of my adult life.

I met Nicole 15 years ago. I immediately recognized her as a wildly intelligent woman with endless energy. A woman of French-Canadian heritage, Nicole is strong, passionate and expressive, not unlike her mother. We bonded over our French ancestry and quickly and easily fell into a symbiotic working relationship. A colleague once defined the two of us as a formidable team, a force majeure.

We worked in a fast-paced office with high expectations and Nicole thrived. I've often observed that she works best under pressure and does her best writing late into the night when there is solitude and silence. When the rest of the world is fast asleep, Nicole can be found banging away at her keyboard. She is formidable, but what truly bonded us as lifelong friends was conflict not harmony. I can't remember the issue, but what I do remember is that I was in some way offended and marched immediately into her office to make my position and sentiment known. I was met with an equally direct response.

The day continued, and after we had walked away and found time to reflect, we reconnected to talk it out. I have told others it was a relationship born of fire but only the most brilliant and lasting gemstones form under heat and pressure. Nicole is undoubtedly a diamond, a dazzling force to behold. When she is in her element I sit back and watch her work. Thanks to her support and mentorship we share a deep connection. Our love and support of each other never wanes or wavers.

Funnily enough, it was Nicole's husband who observed that her longest and closest relationships are formed by fire and conflict. If you haven't experienced and moved past some struggle together, your friendship won't last. Truer words have never been spoken.

To say I love Nicole doesn't do our relationship justice. She possesses every incredible characteristic a person could have. And she has passed the best parts of herself to her two beautiful daughters who are professionals in their own right. We all have our flaws — I have mine and Nicole has hers — but she always strives to improve. Forever reflective, Nicole searches earnestly for ways to be an even better wife, mother, grandmother and friend.

I know I can handle anything life throws at me because I have such a strong foundation of people, including Nicole, in my corner. I believe the Creator brings people into your life for a reason, and she brought Nicole and me together to be a solid foundation for each other in good times and bad.

Nicole made me understand that people, including family, do not have authority over our lives and should not be allowed to harm us just because they are family. By cutting out the poisonous people in my life she taught me to prioritize myself.

My relationship with Nicole is powerful — I feel it. It transcends distance and time. We have bonded over so many things, large and small, like the growth of her daughters and the adoption of my daughter, animals and so many other things that bring us joy, contentment, and at times, uncontrollable fits of laughter.

This relationship is built on and nurtured by genuine respect, complete trust and above all, love.

Next to my grandmother and my mother, Nicole is the most important woman in my life. All three women provided me with a strong moral compass and a sense of personal power that has allowed me to navigate the world both personally and professionally. My friendship with Nicole has taught me how to connect with my emotions and my power, and that I have the strength to achieve anything: I am only limited by my imagination.

It is my wish that every woman can support, nurture and guide other women in their efforts to achieve contentment in every aspect of their lives. Nicole has done all of that for me. I only hope to be able to pay it forward to bring foundational change to other women in my life.

This brings me to my third life lesson: surround yourself with like-minded, supportive women. Seek them out, make them part of your circle and soar! Choose your role models carefully. If you do, there is nothing you can't achieve with incredible women in your corner.

Thank you, Nicole, for being my friend, my confidante, my mentor, my sister. There is no one in the world like you — always be you.

Je t'aime!

Tracy Allen

Project Manager

I am married to a wonderful man and am a mother and grandmother. I am a project manager with over 33 years of experience in human resources, which serves me well in the delivery of complex, multi-faceted knowledge projects. In these 33 years I have worked with incredible women who exemplify the words 'friend' and 'leader.' Working and observing these women, I found my own voice, discovered my own strength and an inner fortitude I used to help me realize personal and professional goals.

I value all my relationships. They range from the ones I have had since I was five years-old, to more recent relationships of four and five years. My circle is wide, diverse. Every relationship is as unique and brilliant as the woman I call friend. I have known this author for more than 14 years and am honoured to contribute to these collective works. Merci!

The Healing Power of Friendship: Through Tough Times

Nicole van Kuppeveld

Time went both fast and slow from the discovery of my 'accidental' aneurysm to the surreal conversation in the neurosurgeon's office where he said: "Three things can happen. The aneurysm will burst and you will die instantly. The aneurysm will burst and you will make it to the hospital, we will do surgery and you will most likely be left with some level of permanent cognitive or physical impairment. Or if you make it to the surgery date and through the surgery you will have no impairments and will go on and live your life."

That was October 2017. I remember the fall and Christmas seasons of that year with great clarity. You take in all those little details and individual moments because you are keenly aware they could be your last.

In December, sitting by the Christmas tree, I wrote letters to my spouse, my two young adult daughters and to the GEMS in my collection. These letters captured my fondest memories, conveyed the lessons I'd learned in my life and captured deep emotions related to the gratitude I'd felt for those most dear to me. Through the tears, I poured out my soul into those love letters. Strangely, sharing left me with a sense of peace, knowing that if the surgery did not go well, my husband, daughters and those friends would get a copy of these letters. They would not be left wondering and would know how precious they were and what they meant to me in my life. That they were my life.

My brain surgery took place on March 2, 2018.

It was touching to be surrounded pre-surgically by my mum, husband, two daughters, and one of the most precious gems in my friendship collection. Under the care of a very gifted neurosurgeon, the 1.4-cm diameter stent was put in my brain. After a 24-hour stay, I was discharged home with instructions that I was not to be left unattended for two full weeks.

Gavin took time off work for a few days to support my rest and recovery. Then, our village of family and friends responded to the call to take a shift to watch over me when he returned to work. Each gifted me with their time and was fully present with me during their 'shift' over those two weeks, each in their unique way leaving a precious memory of that special time.

Lauren, my youngest daughter, informed the Dean of Veterinary Medicine, who discouraged her from taking a couple of days from her studies, that she was not asking for permission; she was letting him know she was going home to be with her mum.

Sarah, my eldest daughter, was fully present, showing up for her shift, in her calm, comforting, caring and therapeutic manner. Following along as the conversation shifted from the mundane to delving into those deep questions about the gift that is our life, as I dozed in and out during the conversation.

Monica, my long-ago Girl Guiding buddy, brought a huge pot of homemade pasta soup (enough, of course, for a few meals) and read to me from my paperback until I dozed off for a wee nap.

Karen, my new colleague friend who would later become my business partner, brought along some of her famous candied nut mixture and homemade cookies. As a professional social worker she had the knack for communicating with me in a caring, kind, compassionate, positive and supportive manner that resulted in me eventually drifting off for another nap.

My mum, who knew just what to do to make me feel loved and cherished, was so relieved that I'd come through the surgery she could not do enough. There was so much tenderness in those acts of care it was palpable.

Kim brought the biggest stash of magazines, sweet treats, salty treats (her thing) and her bubbly personality. Our conversations alternated from deep to light with both of us visibly relieved that all had gone well. We made all kinds of plans for the future and our friendship pact deepened.

Denise, a friend from high school with whom I had reconnected through a mutual friend, came to sit with me in her warm, quiet, unassuming way. She brought me the most beautiful willow floral arrangement that captured her exquisite taste and creativity.

Nancy launched her natural caregiver mode into overdrive, lavishing me with her laughter and love. Fussing energetically about my comfort and then, sitting peacefully watching me sleep.

Melanie, a dear friend I had met through my service league, came and our conversation focused on every detail of the surgery and the amazing technology that allowed the surgeon to put a stent in my brain with a catheter via my femoral artery.

Ian, my friend and training partner, finally looked relaxed after not having slept well between my date of diagnosis and our post-surgery visit. We eagerly anticipated and counted down the days until we could safely resume our three-times-a-week training regime as per the surgeon's orders.

TD, another precious friend, who cared for and lost her mum too early, came by to share her time and love. We talked about those who had gone too soon and reminded ourselves of the precious gift of life we are given each day.

Monica, my childhood friend, called to express immense relief that I'd made it through with flying colours. We spent time reminiscing about our friendship memories from four decades. It felt good to be wrapped in her warmth and love.

My colleagues, writers' group, service club members and friends from many of my social circles came by for short visits. They sent beautiful bouquets, called, brought meals or wrote handwritten notes. My husband's employer, who likely felt some remorse about him having to return to work after only a few days post-op, sent the biggest get-well basket we had ever seen, which each of my 'sitters' explored, pulling out a favourite to share or take home!

When my potentially life-altering surgery was a distant memory and the COVID pandemic was deemed officially over, 2023 arrived. It was the worst year of my life. I was struggling with a serious health issue, an unknown allergen that was triggering anaphylactic shock, my mum was struggling with her decision to put my dad, whose dementia was progressing, into care, and my group coaching and leadership development consultancy was failing.

Honestly, without a close circle of friends who had experienced similar personal struggles being there to listen while I poured out my feelings, without them holding the space for me to see a way forward, without them allowing me to be the rawest and most vulnerable version of myself I am not sure how I would have gotten through that year!

I share with you these two stories to point out the importance of investing in your friendships. All of the years that I had spent cultivating and tending my friendships paid out in spades. I felt so nurtured, supported and cared for during two of the most difficult periods in my life. And the other key takeaway was to give myself permission to ask for support in a time of great fear, pain and vulnerability.

Friendship is about being there for each other.

I was there for them during tough periods in their lives. They were here for me during my difficult months and days. And I will be there for them — and they for me unconditionally in all of those dark times that will inevitably come. Having friends who are there for you lightens the load. They remind us that "This too shall pass." (13th century Sufi poets) "That which doesn't kill us will make us stronger." (German philosopher Friedrich Nietzsche, 1888) and that "It is always darkest before the dawn." (English historian and theologian Thomas Fuller, 1650)

And that, in the words of Carole King: "All you gotta do is call out my name and I'll come running. Yes, I will. You got a friend."

A Tribute

Writing a book is a big undertaking.

Writing it with friends as your co-authors makes it doable and like any friendship adventure, you grow from the shared experience and create a lasting memory.

I started this friendship adventure by extending an invitation to close friends to share inspirational stories about their friendships.

It was a big ask.

Only two amongst us are professional writers and although everyone has a friendship story not everyone wants to share it publicly. Not everyone has the time. For some, the pressure or the fear of not getting it right or disappointing me or our readers (you) was daunting. Some had too much going on in their lives to focus on or dedicate time to this friendship project. Perhaps their version of our friendship is different from my version. Or at some level, perhaps they did not believe they had something valuable to contribute. Some did not see it as a priority. There are probably as many reasons to decline as there were those to whom I extended the invitation to participate.

At the end of my compelling invitation I told them that whether they accepted this invitation to participate or not, I would respect their decision and would still love them. I relish being real and authentic, so their straight responses and sharing their feelings, time constraints and or their current struggles were appreciated. I respect their decision and it will not change the nature of our friendship in any way.

Twenty-one friends agreed to co-author this friendship anthology.

Those who said yes have earned some additional space in my heart. At some level, they did it for me, for our friendship and for the benefit of those who are struggling to develop the kinds of friendship that we share. I will forever be grateful for their stories that will make you laugh and make you cry, stories of the ways they have cultivated deep friendships. About how to show up as a friend and to find friends who love you in your brilliance and imperfections at the same time. The depth of the wisdom and the teaching in these stories are touching reflections of how to create connections that feed the soul.

It took courage.

They pushed through their individual fears. They reached out for support and shared honestly the impact that this important but daunting task was having on them. Some lost sleep. Some developed tension, the cumulation of that pressure to deliver held somewhere in their bodies. I understand some F-Bombs were used, attached to my name at pressure points in the project timeline. There was a 24-hour press pause with one of the co-authors who was committed but threatening to drop out. One tried to woo me into a lunch date to let me know she was going to drop out (after the dropout date). After our pep talk and a chapter outline during lunch, she was back on board and wrote an amazing story. Another friend from across the digital ocean was ready to jump ship and needed to hear that her story provides insights for those who have difficulty establishing intimate friendships.

They each found their writer's voice and each one has produced a unique and compelling story of how to forge lasting friendships.

As their stories evolved, with the support of motivational and writing coaching from Keri and Nancy, they grew in confidence. They were gently encouraged to reach deeper, to tell their stories more authentically. Their stories are powerful and my hope is that at least one or more will resonate with you as a reader. Hopefully their chapters will illustrate how they needed to show up differently to cultivate, nurture and sustain the kinds of friendships they have in their lives.

Although some days it felt like herding cats, my role was to bring out the best in them, to hold a space for them to be able to pull up their story from deep inside themselves, to cheer them on, to work alongside them in solidarity as I wrote my chapters. There were intense moments and strong feelings like relief and joy when the chapters were submitted, as well as frustration and disillusionment when their thoughts were not translating into riveting stories. There were differences of opinion about important things like what should be kept out of a friendship anthology, about what took away from the strong themes and powerful messages and what enhanced and strengthened their stories. Those who indicated they were 'in' honoured their commitment and delivered on their promise.

If you asked each of them, they would tell you they grew, in different ways, from this experience. That writing allowed them to remember friendships from their past and reignite warm memories. That they developed some new skills. That they learned things about themselves. About our friendship. That they really are friendship experts in their own right, as each of them has been able to cultivate long-lasting friendships that feed their soul.

I will forever be grateful and treasure this book's co-authors, 20 women and one man, who are the most brilliant GEMS in my friendship collection.

A special human on our friendship anthology adventure was Keri Sweetman, who is an amazing motivational coach, editor and writing guide who assisted us in creating this remarkable anthology. She encouraged us to take our storytelling to a deeper level, resulting in 'a resource full of wisdom, emotion, and love" In her foreword, she made a compelling case for sharing inspirational stories, like the ones in this friendship anthology. We are deeply grateful for the interest, effort and love she invested. As for me, I am delighted to have deepened my friendships during this extraordinary learning process.

With much love,
Nicole

Appendix A: Reflection & Book Club Questions

Each author provided thought provoking questions for you to use as personal reflections. These reflection questions can also be used for book club discussions. We hope they will be helpful in your continued journey to cultivate, nurture and sustain new and existing friendships.

Chapter 1 : Seeking Connections: Being True to Yourself

Desired Qualities: What are the qualities in a friend that are most important to you? How do these qualities contribute to the overall strength of the connection? How do they contribute to moving from acquaintances to friends?

Authentic Connection: How do you define an authentic friendship? What qualities or behaviours contribute to the authenticity of a connection? How can we cultivate authenticity in our friendships?

Chapter 2 : Forty Nine Years and Counting: The Enduring Magic of a True Connection

Enduring Bonds: How does this story illustrate the enduring power of lifelong friendships? What qualities contribute to such strong bonds?

Support and Encouragement: How have the author and Nicole supported each other through life's challenges? What qualities make a supportive and encouraging friend?

Chapter 3: Cherished Memories: Timeless Moments

Shared Together

Childhood Friendships: Can you recall specific moments or experiences from your childhood that have shaped your current friendships? How have these early connections influenced your understanding of the importance of friendship?

Changing Friendships: How have your childhood friendships changed or evolved over time? What factors have contributed to the enduring nature of these connections, even after years of separation?

Chapter 4: Reconnecting with A Sunflowers Radiance

Volunteering and Community Involvement: How have shared experiences, such as volunteering together, strengthened their bond? How can volunteering help you meet new people and form friendships?

Gratitude and Appreciation: How can you cultivate an attitude of gratitude in your own friendships? What are you most grateful for in your friendships? Write a short note or message to a friend expressing your appreciation for them.

Chapter 5: A Perspective

Impact on Identity: How can you truly understand and appreciate what friends have meant to you over your life? How have friendships shaped your identity and worldview? Have they influenced your values, beliefs or aspirations?

Sharing and Communicating: How do you communicate how friends have moved, touched and inspired you? How can you effectively express gratitude and appreciation for your friends?

Chapter 6: From Russia to Canada with Love

Finding Friendship: Why are friendships so important to Nadia? How do her friendships contribute to her overall well-being? What role have friendships played when you have moved to a new country, city or community?

Female Friendship: How does Nadia's story highlight the strength and importance of female friendships? What unique qualities do women bring to their friendships? How can we foster stronger friendships with other women in our communities? What can we learn from Nadia's experiences?

Chapter 7: You Contain Multitudes: Calling on Our Masculine and Feminine Qualities to Deepen Friendships

Diversity and Inclusion: How has this friendship story helped you appreciate and understand the importance of diversity and inclusion? How can we promote diversity and inclusion in our own friendships? What lessons have you learned about the value of different perspectives?

Personal Growth: What have you learned about yourself through your interactions with friends?How can we use our friendships to challenge our own beliefs and perspectives? What role can friends play in helping us grow and evolve as individuals?

Chapter 8: Close Friends

Psychology and Friendship: Why are researchers in the field of psychology so interested in studying the elements and outcomes of friendship? Are there any specific psychological theories or frameworks that you find particularly relevant to understanding friendships?

Friendship Components: In your experience, what are the most important components of a friendship? How do your own views on friendship components compare to the findings of psychological research?

Chapter 9: Nurturing Intergenerational Friendships

Intergenerational Connections: What have you learned about building friendship across generations? How have your intergenerational connections challenged your assumptions about age and friendship?

Breaking Down Barriers: What challenges or stereotypes did you face when forming an intergenerational friendship? How can we encourage others to break down barriers and form friendships with people from different generations?

Chapter 10: Friendship Reflections: Looking Back and Moving Forward

Difficult Times: How does the author illustrate the importance of friends during difficult times? Recall an experience where a friend provided support during a difficult time in your life.

Overcoming Challenges: How did Nicole's friendships provide her with support and encouragement during challenging times? What role can friends play in helping us navigate challenges and overcome adversity?

Chapter 11: Walking and Talking: The Essence of Being Vulnerable

Friendship and Well-being: How have your friendships contributed to your overall well-being and quality of life? What positive impact have these behaviours had on your physical, mental and emotional health?

Fostering Friendships: What do you believe are the essential qualities or behaviours that foster long-lasting friendships? What factors have contributed to the enduring nature of your connection with forever friends? Can you recall specific moments or experiences that have deepened your connection with friends?

Chapter 12: Dementia's Journey: A United Front for Person-Centred Care

Advocacy and Activism: What motivates you to speak out and take action? How can we become more effective advocates with our friends for the issues we care about? What role has community involvement or advocacy played in your friendships?

Resilience and Support: How have you and your friends supported each other through personal losses? What strategies can we use to offer comfort, encouragement, and a listening ear to friends who are struggling? What role has resilience and forgiveness played in maintaining your friendship?

Chapter 13: The Mystery and Profound Impact of Friendships

Trust and Vulnerability: How does the author connect trust and vulnerability to strong friendships? How can you create a safe space for vulnerability with your friends? What role does vulnerability play in building strong connections?

The Power of Giving: The author emphasizes the importance of giving freely in friendships. How can you incorporate more generosity into your friendships? Are you giving your friends the time that is needed to cultivate your friendship?

Chapter 14: Finding a Pet Sitter and a Sister Friend

The Power of Serendipity: What role do chance encounters and unexpected connections play in your friendship? How can we be more open to serendipitous encounters and the potential for new friendships to develop?

Depth of Human Connection: How can we foster empathy and understanding in our relationships? What can we do to create a safe and supportive environment for open and honest communication? How can we cultivate deeper and more meaningful connections with the people in our lives?

Chapter 15: Kindred Spirits of the Digital Ocean

Virtual Friendships: How does this story challenge your perceptions about forming deep friendships in the digital age? Can genuine connections truly develop online?

Shared Disappointments: How did the shared experience of disappointment bring Betty and Nicole together? Can shared adversity strengthen bonds?

Chapter 16: A Rare Gem

Bonding: Do you believe strong bonds can form solely through online interactions? How can you find common ground with online friends to foster deeper connections?

Resilience and Growth: Despite challenges, Nicole and Zyrha's relationship thrived. What qualities do you believe contributed to their resilience and ability to grow together?

Chapter 17: Workout Buddies to Soulmates: Unexpected Shared Experiences

Challenge and Grow: How do friendships challenge and help you grow as a person? Can you think of a time when a friend challenged your perspective and helped you see things differently?

Aging and Age Differences: Have you let age be a barrier to creating intergenerational friendships? How can we maintain strong friendship connections as we age?

Chapter 18: Lifelong Allies

Shared Experiences: How have your shared experiences with your friends, such as volunteering together, contributed to the depth and richness of your friendship? Can you identify specific areas where your beliefs and perspectives align with your friends?

Life Stages: How have your friendships evolved at different life stages? Have your priorities changed over time, and how has this impacted your friendships? How have you navigated the challenges and changes that have occurred in your lives as friends?

Chapter 19: More Than Family: The Deep Connection Between Mother and Daughter

Family as Friends: What does this story teach us about the enduring nature of love? How do we shift beyond family ties to friendships? How can we foster lifelong connections with our loved ones?

Mother-Daughter Friendships: How does the author's relationship with her daughter illustrate the unique bond between mothers and daughters? What can mothers and daughters learn from this story about evolving their relationship into a friendship?

Chapter 20: Just Say Yes!

Growth and Development: How have your friendships contributed to your personal growth and development? Have there been specific experiences or challenges within your friendships that have led to significant self-discovery

Lessons Learned and Future Aspirations: What are the most important lessons you have learned about friendship throughout your life? How do you hope to nurture and deepen your existing friendships in the future?

Chapter 21: A Blend of Shared Experiences and Laughter

Shared Values: What are the core values the author identifies as important in her friendships? What values do you prioritize in your friendships? Can you recall a time when shared values helped you connect with someone?

Humorous Incidents: What role does humour play in your friendships? Can you think of a funny experience you've shared with a friend that strengthened your bond?

Chapter 22: Creating Close Friendships Through Safe Spaces

Sharing is Caring: How have your friendships allowed you to show your caring? And how has sharing lightened your load? What positive impact have these relationships had on your mental and emotional health?

Strengths and Weaknesses: What are your strengths and weaknesses as a friend? How do these qualities contribute to your interactions with friends? Are there any areas where you would like to improve your friendship skills?

Chapter 23: A Legacy of Love: Lessons from Extraordinary Women

Work Friends: How have your shared experiences, such as working together and navigating work challenges, deepened your friendships? Can you recall specific instances where shared work experiences have strengthened your bonds?

Fire and Forgiveness: How do you address differences of opinion and conflict in your friendships? Can you share a specific instance where you had to forgive or let go of something? How did this experience impact your friendships?

Chapter 24: The Healing Power of Friendship: Through Tough Times

Fun Activities: Can you recall specific instances where engaging in fun activities together has strengthened your bonds? Are there any new activities you'd like to explore with your friends in the future?

Nurturing Friendships: What lessons can readers take away from the author's experiences with friendship? How can these lessons be applied to your own relationships? How can we prioritize and nurture our friendships?

In Memoriam: Denise Robert 1964-2021

"The only way to have a friend is to be one."
—Ralph Waldo Emerson

Are you ready to transform your friendships and deepen your connections? Dive into Creating Connections: How Friendships Feed the Soul, today.

Join Nicole van Kuppeveld and 21 of her inspiring friends as they share heartfelt stories and invaluable insights that will guide you on your journey to building meaningful friendships. Whether you're looking to forge new bonds or strengthen existing ones, this anthology is packed with wisdom, humour and life lessons.

Start enriching your life with the beauty of true friendship. Creating Connections: How Friendships Feed the Soul will help you take the next step toward creating deeper connections with the people you value most in your life. Join us on a journey of cultivating, fostering and sustaining friendships.

Copies of this friendship anthology will soon be available at Amazon.ca and Amazon.com

To learn more about the co-authors, to join a friendship circle or to learn more about women's leadership visit

https://creatingconnectionsfriendshipsthatfeedthesoul.ca/

Manufactured by Amazon.ca
Bolton, ON

41398104R00103